W9-AKB-825

OPPOSING VIEWPOINTS® SERIES

Nanotechnology

Jacqueline Langwith, Book Editor

GREENHAVEN PRESS
A part of Gale, Cengage Learning

Detroit • New York • San Francisco • New Haven, Conn • Waterville, Maine • London

Christine Nasso, *Publisher*
Elizabeth Des Chenes, *Managing Editor*

© 2010 Greenhaven Press, a part of Gale, Cengage Learning.

Gale and Greenhaven Press are registered trademarks used herein under license.

For more information, contact:
Greenhaven Press
27500 Drake Rd.
Farmington Hills, MI 48331-3535
Or you can visit our Internet site at gale.cengage.com

For product information and technology assistance, contact us at

Gale Customer Support, 1-800-877-4253
For permission to use material from this text or product, submit all requests online at
www.cengage.com/permissions

Further permissions questions can be emailed to permissionrequest@cengage.com

Articles in Greenhaven Press anthologies are often edited for length to meet page require-ments. In addition, original titles of these works are changed to clearly present the main thesis and to explicitly indicate the author's opinion. Every effort is made to ensure that Greenhaven Press accurately reflects the original intent of the authors. Every effort has been made to trace the owners of copyrighted material.

Cover photograph © Redseal/Photodisc/Getty Images.

LIBRARY OF CONGRESS CATALOGING-IN-PUBLICATION DATA

Nanotechnology / Jacqueline Langwith, book editor.
    p. cm. -- (Opposing viewpoints)
    Includes bibliographical references and index.
    978-0-7377-4386-9 (hardcover)
    978-0-7377-4385-2 (pbk.)
    1. Nanotechnology. 2. Nanotechnology--Moral and ethical aspects. 3. Nano-structured materials. I. Langwith, Jacqueline.
    T174.7.N3684 2009
    620'.5--dc22

                                         2009019786

Printed in the United States of America
1 2 3 4 5 6 7 13 12 11 10 09

Contents

Chapter 3: What Are the Implications of Nanomedicine?

Chapter 4: What Role Should the U.S. Play in Promoting or Regulating Nanotechnology?

Why Consider
Opposing Viewpoints?

> *"The only way in which a human being can make some approach to knowing the whole of a subject is by hearing what can be said about it by persons of every variety of opinion and studying all modes in which it can be looked at by every character of mind. No wise man ever acquired his wisdom in any mode but this."*
>
> *John Stuart Mill*

In our media-intensive culture it is not difficult to find differing opinions. Thousands of newspapers and magazines and dozens of radio and television talk shows resound with differing points of view. The difficulty lies in deciding which opinion to agree with and which "experts" seem the most credible. The more inundated we become with differing opinions and claims, the more essential it is to hone critical reading and thinking skills to evaluate these ideas. Opposing Viewpoints books address this problem directly by presenting stimulating debates that can be used to enhance and teach these skills. The varied opinions contained in each book examine many different aspects of a single issue. While examining these conveniently edited opposing views, readers can develop critical thinking skills such as the ability to compare and contrast authors' credibility, facts, argumentation styles, use of persuasive techniques, and other stylistic tools. In short, the Opposing Viewpoints Series is an ideal way to attain the higher-level thinking and reading skills so essential in a culture of diverse and contradictory opinions.

In addition to providing a tool for critical thinking, Opposing Viewpoints books challenge readers to question their own strongly held opinions and assumptions. Most people form their opinions on the basis of upbringing, peer pressure, and personal, cultural, or professional bias. By reading carefully balanced opposing views, readers must directly confront new ideas as well as the opinions of those with whom they disagree. This is not to simplistically argue that everyone who reads opposing views will—or should—change his or her opinion. Instead, the series enhances readers' understanding of their own views by encouraging confrontation with opposing ideas. Careful examination of others' views can lead to the readers' understanding of the logical inconsistencies in their own opinions, perspective on why they hold an opinion, and the consideration of the possibility that their opinion requires further evaluation.

Evaluating Other Opinions

To ensure that this type of examination occurs, Opposing Viewpoints books present all types of opinions. Prominent spokespeople on different sides of each issue as well as well-known professionals from many disciplines challenge the reader. An additional goal of the series is to provide a forum for other, less known, or even unpopular viewpoints. The opinion of an ordinary person who has had to make the decision to cut off life support from a terminally ill relative, for example, may be just as valuable and provide just as much insight as a medical ethicist's professional opinion. The editors have two additional purposes in including these less known views. One, the editors encourage readers to respect others' opinions—even when not enhanced by professional credibility. It is only by reading or listening to and objectively evaluating others' ideas that one can determine whether they are worthy of consideration. Two, the inclusion of such viewpoints encourages the important critical thinking skill of objectively evaluating an author's credentials and bias. This evaluation will illuminate an author's reasons for taking a particular stance on an issue and will aid in readers' evaluation of the author's ideas.

It is our hope that these books will give readers a deeper understanding of the issues debated and an appreciation of the complexity of even seemingly simple issues when good and honest people disagree. This awareness is particularly important in a democratic society such as ours in which people enter into public debate to determine the common good. Those with whom one disagrees should not be regarded as enemies but rather as people whose views deserve careful examination and may shed light on one's own.

Thomas Jefferson once said that "difference of opinion leads to inquiry, and inquiry to truth." Jefferson, a broadly educated man, argued that "if a nation expects to be ignorant and free . . . it expects what never was and never will be." As individuals and as a nation, it is imperative that we consider the opinions of others and examine them with skill and discernment. The Opposing Viewpoints Series is intended to help readers achieve this goal.

David L. Bender and Bruno Leone,
Founders

Introduction

> *"It would be very easy to make an analysis of any complicated chemical substance; all one would have to do would be to look at it and see where the atoms are. The only trouble is that the electron microscope is one hundred times too poor."*
>
> Richard Feynman,
> *"There's Plenty of Room at the Bottom," December 29, 1959.*

Richard Feynman is famous in nanotechnology lore. Many people credit his talk on December 29, 1959, to the annual gathering of the American Physical Society as the beginning of nanotechnology. In his talk, "There's Plenty of Room at the Bottom," Feynman said scientists should focus their attention on "manipulating and controlling things at the small scale." Things at the nanoscale are so small they're measured in nanometers, a unit equal to one billionth of a meter. In order to visualize these objects, Feynman said the best microscope of the time—the electron microscope—would have to be improved 100 times so that individual atoms could be visualized. A microscope that could see individual atoms would help scientists answer many fundamental questions, asserted Feynman. It would take more than 20 years to develop the type of microscope Feynman was explaining. It wasn't until the development of this microscope and other even more advanced microscopes that the field of nanotechnology finally took off. The inventions of the scanning tunneling microscope (STM) and the atomic force microscope (AFM) in the 1980s are two of the most important developments in the field of nanotechnology.

Humankind has always wanted to see beyond its own sight, whether it is to see the far away or to discern the very small. The earliest forerunner to the powerful telescopes and microscopes in use today was invented in Middleburg, Holland, in the latter part of the 16th century. Debate exists about who invented it first, but either father and son team Zaccharias and Hans Janssen, or Hans Lippershey—all watchmakers—are reported to have placed multiple eye glass lenses in a tube and realized that objects placed in front of the tube appeared enlarged when viewed from the back of the tube. The Dutchmen's crude instrument was the prototype for the telescopes used by Galileo Galilei and others to observe the moon and the planets in our solar system. The contraption was also used as the prototype for the optical microscopes used by Robert Hooke in 1665 to prepare his famous book *Micrographia* and later by Antony van Leeuwenhoek to observe bacteria, blood cells, yeast, insects, and many other tiny organisms.

Optical microscopes, like those used by Hooke and Leeuwenhoek, were used for hundreds of years to reveal to the human eye the intricate details of the heretofore invisible. Optical microscopes are also called light microscopes because they use visible light and a system of lenses to magnify images. There are two basic kinds of optical microscopes. Simple optical microscopes use one lens, while compound optical microscopes use two or more lenses to view objects. Hooke used a compound microscope to view specimens, while Leeuwenhoek used a simple microscope. Light microscopes can generally magnify images up to 2,000 times.

The electron microscope, invented in 1931, is 1,000 times better than the optical microscope. An electron microscope depends on a beam of electrons rather than light to view an object. The first electron microscope was built in 1931 by German engineers Ernst Ruska and Max Knoll. Ruska won the Nobel Prize in Physics for the invention in 1986. Although their initial instrument was capable of magnifying objects by only four hundred times, it demonstrated the principles of electron microscopy. Modern electron microscopes can achieve magnifications of 2 million times, but they are still based upon Ruska's and Knoll's prototype.

Scientists needing to see the very small depended solely on the electron microscope for some fifty years, and it is still a staple in many laboratories. Researchers use basic electron microscopes to examine biological materials, large molecules, medical biopsy samples, metals, crystalline structures, and the characteristics of various surfaces. No matter how useful the basic electron microscope is, however, it cannot see individual atoms and nanosized particles. So in 1959, when Feynman gave his speech, nanotechnology was a concept that could not be tested. Scientists could only imagine what was going on at the nanoscale level, but they could not see it. The ability to peer into the nano realm and see individual atoms was finally provided in 1981 with the invention of the scanning tunneling microscope.

Gerd Binnig's and Heinrich Rohrer's invention of the scanning tunneling microscope (STM) enabled scientists to obtain nano-scale images and manipulate individual atoms. Scanning tunneling microscopy works by running a tiny slender probe back and forth over a surface creating a three-dimensional representation of the object. Unlike electron and light microscopes, the scanning probe never touches or interacts with the sample. This breakthrough was essential for the development of the field of nanotechnology. What had previously only been imaginable, was now within view and testable.

Another scanning microscope was invented soon after the STM, which further enhanced scientists' ability to visualize nanoscale materials. The STM could only be used with metallic compounds, certain plasmas, salts, and other materials that have the ability to conduct an electric charge. This limited STM's usefulness. A few years after he invented the STM, however, Gerd Binning teamed with Clavin Quate and Christopher Berger to invent the atomic force microscope (AFM), which was also a scanning microscope. The AFM can be used with conductive and non-conductive materials so it has much broader use. It further enhanced scientists' ability to manipulate atoms and molecules.

The STM and AFM are commonly called the "eyes of nanotechnology." Their development enabled the rapid burgeoning of the nanotechnology industry. At first these microscopes were only available to a few scientists who had the resources and the ability to construct them. Once STMs and AFMs became commercially available more scientists were able to use them and they are now a common tool for any scientist involved in nanotechnology research.

Scientists are generally in agreement that the inventions of the STM and the AFM are the two most important enabling developments in the field of nanotechnology. This may be one of the few issues where nanotechnology scientists are in consensus. In *Opposing Viewpoints: Nanotechnology*, scientists, policy makers, ethicists, and others contribute their viewpoints on a number of controversial issues in the following chapters: What Are the Benefits of Nanotechnology? What Are the Implications of Molecular Nanotechnology? What Are the Implications of Nanomedicine? and What Role Should the U.S. Government Play in Promoting or Regulating Nanotechnology?

OPPOSING
VIEWPOINTS®
SERIES

What Are the Benefits Of Nanotechnology?

Chapter Preface

Scientists are using nanotechnology in surprising ways to enhance common consumer products. Antimicrobial socks and stain resistant pants were two of the first consumer products to incorporate nanotechnology. Nanotech socks contain nanosized particles of silver, which kill bacteria and fungi. Stain resistant pants contain billions of whisker-like nanosized fibers, which whisk liquids away from the surface of the pants. In addition to these innovations, researchers are exploring hundreds of other ways that nanotechnology can enhance consumer products. One area receiving a lot of attention from scientists is using nanotechnology to enhance food products. Many people believe that nanotechnologies can make food healthier, safer to eat, longer lasting, and better tasting. Many other people, however, are worried about the health risks of food products containing nanoparticles.

Nanotechnology can make nutritious food more appealing to kids and make less nutritious foods, like milkshakes and Coca-Cola, more nutritious and healthy. In a 2009 article in *Nanowerk*, Dutch food scientist Frans Kampers explains that nanotechnology allows the "re-engineering of ingredients to bring healthy nutrients more efficiently to the body while allowing less-desirable components to pass on through." For instance, Kampers's fellow researchers at Holland's Wageningen University are using nanotechnology to make low-fat, but good tasting mayonnaise. The nanomayonnaise consists of an emulsion of tiny droplets that are composed of water on the inside and oil on the outside. What you taste is the oil, and it tastes just like regular mayonnaise. Since the inner part of the droplet contains water, however, there is far less fat in the mayonnaise. Other scientists are researching nanomilk that has the texture and taste of real milk, nanocanola oil that blocks cholesterol from entering the bloodstream, and na-nomilkshakes that are more nutritious *and* better tasting than regular milkshakes.

While making foods more nutritious or better tasting is a primary goal for many scientists, other scientists are focusing on the use of nanotechnology to enhance the plastics and other materials in which food is packaged. Some scientists en-vision a day when food packaging will be able to respond to environmental conditions, repair itself, alert a consumer to contamination, and release preservatives or antibacterial agents. An example of nanoenhanced food packaging, which is already in use, is ripeSense, a ripeness detector produced in New Zealand. RipeSense works by reacting to the aromas re-leased as fruits and vegetables ripen. The sensor is initially red and turns orange and finally yellow as fruits or vegetables ripen. "Clearly, nanotechnology offers tremendous opportuni-ties for innovative developments in food packaging that can benefit both consumers and industry," says Robert Brackett of the Grocery Manufacturers Association.

Where some see the potential benefits of using nanotech-nology in the food industry, others see the potential risks. The very characteristic that makes nanotechnology so useful, that particles smaller than 100 nanometers behave differently than their large-scale counterparts, is also the thing that makes it risky. Organizations like the Friends of the Earth (FOE) are worried about the risks of ingesting nanosized particles with the ability to pass through cell membranes and exert unfore-seen effects. In their report *Out of the Laboratory and onto Our Plates*, the FOE explains "the potential for ingested non-degradable nanoparticles to cause long-term pathological ef-fects in addition to short-term toxicity is of great concern." According to the FOE, "nanomaterials now in commercial use by the food industry, such as nanotitanium dioxide, silver, zinc, and zinc oxide have been shown to be toxic to cells and tissues in *in vitro* experiments and to test animals in *in vivo* studies." Journalist Francesca Levy agrees. In *Business Week's* online debate room she says, "if nanoparticles can do this much damage when inhaled or injected, the ones we eat could have unforeseen consequences. Our limited understanding of this technology should give manufacturers pause." Many groups, organizations, and scientists believe that before nanotechnology is used in food and food packaging, further research is needed to understand the unanticipated behavior of ingested nanoparticles.

The debate over nanotech foods is just one of the issues surrounding nanotechnology, where some people see benefits, while others see risks. In the following chapter, the contributors debate the potential benefits and risks of nanotechnology to the environment, to global equity, and to society in general.

"It [nanotechnology] is a real, very
broadly based and multidisciplinary
area of human endeavour and not just
a token epithet that can be applied to
the latest research proposal or business
venture."

Nanotechnology Has the Potential to Provide Significant Benefits Despite Concerns

Roger W. Whatmore

In the following viewpoint, Roger W. Whatmore asserts that despite some concerns, nanotechnology can provide huge benefits to society. Whatmore describes how the field of nanotechnology began in 1959 when physicist Richard Feynman gave a lecture describing the technological advantages of working with things on a very small scale. Feynman's lecture eventually lead to a diverse set of nanotechnologies, such as tiny machines called microelectromechanical systems, coatings made of carbon nanotubes, and nanosized particles that behave differently than their larger-sized counterparts. After describing what nanotechnologies are and

Roger W. Whatmore, "Nanotechnology—Should We Be Worried?" *Nanotechnology Perceptions*, vol. 1, July 2005, pp. 67–77. Copyright © 2005 Collegium Basilea. Reproduced by permission. www.unibas.ch.

their potential to impact our lives, Whatmore asks the question of whether or not society should be worried about this new small technology. He discounts concerns that "molecular assemblers" will one day take over the world, but says some concerns, such as the environmental and health impacts of nanoparticles, are warranted. Despite these concerns, Whatmore believes that nanotechnology is more than a marketing term. He believes it is a useful technology that has the potential to change our lives and impact the world around us. Whatmore is a professor of engineering nanotechnology at Cranfield University in the United Kingdom.

As you read, consider the following questions:

1. According to Whatmore, a nanometer is how many atoms across?

2. According to Whatmore, who first put forward the idea of a "clanking replicator?"

3. According to Whatmore, what did Japanese researcher Sumio Iijima discover in 1991?

From the development of the earliest stone tools to the most sophisticated microprocessor, man has increasingly, and sometimes unwittingly, shaped the world around him through the use of his technologies. These technologies impact upon all aspects of our lives. We depend upon them for the food we eat, our transport and our communications. We rely on them for clean water and an increasingly sophisticated level of healthcare. Whole periods of human history are labelled by reference to the dominant technology of the time—the stone age, the bronze age, the iron age, the industrial age, the computer age. We are all familiar with these terms and use them without thinking about the profound effect that each of the technologies had—both upon the societies that created them and on the planet itself. Frequently, we are not aware of the impacts the older technologies have had on the world in which we now live—for example, stone axes were used to fell the ancient forests that once covered the UK [United Kingdom] and created the downs and pasture that we now recognize as our "green and pleasant land".

This paper will look at one new area of technology—nanotechnology—and attempt to answer the question "Should we be worried—either about what it is doing now or where it is taking us?" I wonder whether a Neolithic farmer stopped to ask himself the same question while he was felling the trees to create a new stretch of farm land for himself and his family.

What Is Nanotechnology?

Before discussing the issue of where nanotechnology is taking us, and whether we should be worried about it, we must try to understand what it is. So, the first question that I would like to address is "What is nanotechnology?" This is not as easy to answer as one might think, because the term encompasses a huge range of activities. Some people think it is not a single type of activity at all, while others think it is just a term that has been invented to allow researchers to extract large amounts of research funds from government funding agencies! ... Some commentators and financial observers—such the finance house Merrill Lynch—have even gone so far as to suggest that the impact of nanotechnology will be so great that the term will be used to describe a new era of world economic growth.

Why all the fuss? What is this phenomenon that everyone is getting so excited about? Personally, I don't like to get too hung-up on hard definitions. People are far too concerned about these—particularly so with nanotechnology. The prefix "nano" comes from the Greek word "nanos" meaning "a dwarf". Hence "nanotechnology" might well simply mean a technology concerned with small things. However, "nano" has also long been used as a prefix in scientific circles to mean one billionth (using billion in its American sense of a one followed by nine zeros). So we have the term "nanogram" for one billionth of a gram and nanometre for one billionth of a metre. A nanometre is exceedingly small—only about 10 atoms across. On that score, we might expect "nanotechnology" to have something to do with technologies that are working, for example, at the nanometre level and this is the general sense in which the term nanotechnology is used today. It is important to distinguish here between nanoscience, which is the study of phenomena at the very small scale, and nanotechnology, which implies an aim to achieve an end that is in some way "useful". The Royal Society [Britain's National Academy of Sciences]/Royal Academy of Engineering Working Group on the subject adopted the following definitions:

Nanoscience is the study of phenomena and manipulation of materials at atomic, molecular and macromolecular scales, where properties differ significantly from those at larger scale.

Nanotechnologies are the design, characterization, production and application of structures, devices and systems by controlling shave and size at nanometre scale.

Feynman's Lecture

The scale of sizes normally discussed for the applicability of nanotechnology is usually less than 100 (nano meters) nm. Nanoscience, arguably, has been around since the early part of the 20th century, while the idea that there might be some technological advantages to be gained by working at the very small scale came much later. It was first put forward by the famous physicist Richard Feynman, when he gave a lecture in 1959 to the American Physical Society entitled "There's plenty of room at the bottom—an invitation to enter a new field of physics". In this lecture—which actually had almost no physics in it but was mainly concerned with the technology of making things—he explored the benefits that might accrue to us if we started manufacturing things on the very small scale. The ideas he put forward were remarkably prescient. For example, he foresaw the techniques that could be used to make large scale integrated circuits and the revolutionary effects that the use of these circuits would have upon computing. He talked about making machines for sequencing genes by reading DNA molecules. He foresaw the use of electron microscopes for writing massive amounts of information in very small areas. He also talked about using mechanical machines to make smaller machines with increasing precision. Interestingly, for a man who went on to win the Nobel Prize in Physics in 1965 for his work in the field of quantum electrodynamics, he hardly mentioned the quantum mechanical effects associated with the making of very small things, although he did talk about using the interactions of quantized spins, a kind of 'spin logic', which is only now being studied. Many of his predictions in that lecture have come true, and all are aspects of what we would now call "nanotechnology", although he did not use the term itself.

Actually, the first use of the term "nanotechnology" was by Norio Taniguchi who, in 1974, gave a talk describing how the dimensional accuracy with which we make things has improved over time. He studied the developments in machining techniques over the period from 1940 until the early 1970s and predicted (correctly as it turned out) that by the late 1980s techniques would have evolved to a degree that dimensional accuracies of better than 100 nm would be achievable. He called this "nanotechnology". . . .

Top-Down Nanotechnology

You will realize from the above that all the early running in the field of nanotechnology was made by physicists and engineers who mainly thought in terms of making things more and more precisely. This means using one machine to make another, usually smaller machine to greater precision, and using machines (frequently very large and expensive machines) to make things which have incredibly precise features defined upon them. We now call this "top-down" nanotechnology. It has led directly to the hugely successful semiconductor and information and communications technology (ICT) industries. . . . We all use advanced microprocessors in our portable computers. These have metal lines written on them that are only 90 nanometres wide and have upwards of 100 million transistors on a single piece of silicon a few millimetres across. They are objects of mind-boggling complexity and yet they are manufactured at incredibly low cost—a few tens of dollars each. The technologies established by the semiconductor industry are also now being applied in the manufacture of tiny micromechanical machines for sensing and actuation. These "microelectromechanical systems" (also known as MEMS) are finding their way into a host of applications, particularly in the automotive and medical fields, where cost and size-based functionality are key factors. We can start to see here the enormous effects that working at the very small scale is having on our world.

Machines That Can "Pick Up" a Single Atom

There were two other themes that Feynman put forward in his lecture. He envisaged the possibility of making machines that could pick up and put down single atoms. Putting particular atoms together in particular combinations would be a new way for making chemical compounds. Feynman did put forward several reasons why atomic manipulation might not work. These included the . . . forces that would make an atom stick to the finger picking it up, so that once picked up it would be virtually impossible to put down, let alone put it in a particular place relative to another atom. This has been called the "sticky fingers problem".

In 1981 Binnig and Rohrer, based at IBM in Zürich, invented the scanning probe microscope. This uses a very sharp metal point scanned over a surface to create images of the atoms in the surface. Incidentally they won the Nobel prize for this work in 1986. In 1989 Don Eigler used the scanning probe microscope to nudge atoms of xenon on a copper surface held at a temperature close to absolute zero to spell out the letters "IBM". Another one of Feynman's predictions had come true, admittedly under very special conditions. Eigler and his group have since done some remarkable work, mainly using the technique to explore basic physical and quantum mechanical phenomena. Jim Gimzewski at IBM used similar techniques to push single molecules around on surfaces. This kind of work with single atoms and molecules is called "extreme nanotechnology".

Clanking Replicators and Grey Goo

Feynman had another vision in 1959, which was of a factory in which billions of very small machine tools were drilling and stamping myriads of tiny mechanical parts, which would then be assembled into larger products. In the late 1980s another worker in California, Eric Drexler, combined these small manufacturing ideas of Feynman with another thought experiment, which had been put forward by John von Neumann in the late 1940s. This was the idea of a mechanical machine—called a "clanking replicator"—that could be programmed to make replicas of itself. All it would need was a supply of raw materials and a source of energy. Those replicas would make more replicas, and the result would be exponential growth in the number of the machines—until either the source of raw materials or the energy was exhausted.

Drexler combined this "clanking replicator" idea with Feynman's to come up with the concept of the "universal assembler", first put forward in his book *Engines of Creation*. The clanking replicator concept is reduced to very small size through the use of mechanical components that are made on the molecular scale. The first assembler would be programmed to make copies of itself by atomic and molecular manipulation. The exponential growth would lead to billions of assemblers that would be programmed to work in concert with each other to build virtually anything required. You could sprinkle a few assemblers onto a heap of garbage and out would come a washing machine! Clearly such a technology would have enormous economic implications, both in terms of material and energy use, effects on employment, etc. Drexler has set up the Foresight Institute in California and has raised large amounts of money for nanotechnology research based on that idea. He also was the first to raise alarm bells about the possibility of the assemblers reproducing out of control and reducing everything to a "grey goo" of tiny machines. There is now a new variant on this vision, which postulates the fusion of nanotechnology with biotechnology to create an assembler that is at least partly biologically based. In this case, the problem becomes one of "green goo" rather than "grey goo", but the outcome is essentially the same. This idea was subsequently hit upon by the author and screenplay writer Michael Crichton who used it in his novel *Prey*, in which a set of assemblers, originally created for medical inspection and subsequently military purposes, goes out of control and starts hunting down and destroying their creators. I will come back to this Drexlerian vision—or rather nightmare—a little later in this article. It has a lot to answer for, apart from pulp fiction.

Nanosized Particles Behave Differently than Bigger-Sized Particles

I would now like to move away from the ideas originally promulgated in Feynman's 1959 lecture. There have been some remarkable developments in materials science and chemistry over the last 15 years or so, particularly where small size plays a big role in determining basic properties. In the field of materials science, size does indeed matter! If we take a piece of a semiconductor less than about 100 nanometres across, then the electrons in them behave differently from in the bulk. For example, the colours of light absorption and emission change. Very small particles (nanoparticles) of materials like cadmium telluride are being used in applications such as the labelling of biological molecules and in new types of displays. These can be made amazingly precisely in size—say 50 nanometres, plus or minus a couple of nanometres—using reasonably standard wet chemical processes.

Very small particles (less than a few hundred nanometres in size) do not scatter visible light. Good absorbers of ultraviolet light such as titanium dioxide are now being made in nanoparticulate form for sunscreens. The fact that the particles are so small means that they are invisible on the skin, while still being highly effective as UV blockers. Very small particles also possess high surface areas per unit of mass. Oxonica, a start-up company from Oxford University, has found that nanoparticles of cerium oxide, when introduced into diesel fuel, act as oxidation catalysts during combustion. This provides improvements in fuel efficiency of up to 10% and reduces the emissions of carbon soot from the engine exhaust.

Fullerenes and Carbon Nanotubes

If we look at other areas of materials science, we see that new forms of carbon have been discovered. Harry Kroto from the University of Sussex, together with Richard Smalley and Robert Curl, discovered the carbon60 molecule in 1985 (and won the Nobel Prize for chemistry in 1996). It is a sphere 0.7 nanometres across that looks like a soccer ball, or the geodesic dome structure pioneered by the 1930s architect Buckminster Fuller, so they called it buckminsterfullerene. It is amusing to note that if you could expand the C60 molecule so that it was the same size as a soccer ball, the soccer ball itself, if blown up by the same factor, would be about half the size of the planet Jupiter!

The so-called fullerenes form a whole family of related structures that possess remarkable physical and chemical properties. If fully fluorinated, the molecules, which can then be thought of as tiny Teflon balls, form one of the best lubricants known. In 1991 Iijima [Japanese researcher Sumio] discovered carbon nanotubes. These are like sheets of graphite rolled into long tubes, each one being terminated by a fullerene group. They also have remarkable properties. They can be either metallic or semiconducting, depending on the precise way in which the carbon atoms are assembled in the tube. The metallic forms have electrical conductivities 1000 times better than that of copper and are now being mixed with polymers to make conducting composite materials for applications such as electromagnetic shielding in mobile telephones and static electricity reduction in cars. They possess mechanical properties that are many times superior to those of steel, bringing the promise of replacing carbon fibres in a whole new generation of high strength composite materials. They have been demonstrated in applications as diverse as supercapacitors for energy storage, field emission devices for flat panel displays and nanometre-sized transistors. Clearly, these nanomaterials hold huge promise for the future.

Nanotechnology Is a Diverse Field

So, what is nanotechnology? Is it a real subject, or is it just, as the cynics would have us believe, a mechanism for extracting funding from gullible government agencies and investors. Firstly, I hope you can see that it is hugely diverse. It employs all the conventional scientific and engineering subjects in order to achieve new applications. It does this through the exploitation of phenomena in which small size is the key to obtaining an exploitable property. Secondly, it is an area of endeavour where there are, as I have tried to illustrate, real and remarkable properties that we can seek to exploit. Thirdly, and increasingly, we are starting to see convergence between different areas of nanotechnology. The size range of interest between a few nanometres and 100 nanometres is one where

The Promise of Nanotechnology

It's a relatively new area of science that has generated excitement worldwide. Working at the nanoscale, scientists today are creating new tools, products, and technologies to address some of the world's biggest challenges, including

- clean, secure, affordable energy

- stronger, lighter, more durable materials

- low-cost filters to provide clean drinking water

- medical devices and drugs to detect and treat diseases more effectively with fewer side effects

- lighting that uses a fraction of the energy

- sensors to detect and identify harmful chemical or biological agents

- techniques to clean up hazardous chemicals in the environment

Because of the promise of nanotechnology to improve lives and to contribute to economic growth, the Federal Government, through the guiding efforts of the U.S. National Nanotechnology Initiative (NNI), is supporting research in nanotechnology. As a result of the NNI research efforts, the United States is a global leader in nanotechnology development.

National Nanotechnology Initiative,
Nanotechnology: Big Things from a Tiny World, *2009.*
www.nano.gov.

many interesting things happen. All sorts of physical properties change and many biological systems function at this length scale. Hence, we are starting to see the use of processes such as electron beam lithography, originally developed for writing very fine scale features on silicon for electronics, being applied for the modification of surfaces on which biological species can be grown in a controlled way. The self-assembling properties of biological systems, such as DNA molecules, can be used to control the organization of objects such as carbon nanotubes, which may ultimately lead to the ability to grow parts of an integrated circuit, rather than having to rely upon expensive top-down techniques. . . .

Should We Be Worried?

We are thus seeing an area that is providing real potential in its applications. Some people have predicted a world market for nanotechnology-related products of billions or trillions of dollars by the end of the decade. There is no doubt that the technology associated with our ability to manipulate matter on the very small scale is already having major impacts on our lives and this impact will only increase. Hence, we should now ask the question that our Neolithic farmer (presumably) didn't: "Should we be worried?" Could the introduction of nanotechnology have unforeseen consequences?

First let's consider the Drexlerian dystopia in which a rogue molecular assembler, ostensibly created for the betterment of mankind via high efficiency, low cost manufacture, goes out of control and reduces everything to a grey (or green) goo. There are many highly rated, first class scientific minds (including Richard Smalley, the Nobel Prize winner referred to earlier) who have asserted that the "assembler" is not possible for all sorts of reasons. These include the "sticky fingers" problem, problems with the storage and transmission of the huge amount of information needed and the vast complexity of the problem, which would be far, far greater than the complexity of a modern microprocessor. They imply that the assembler concept needs to stay where it belongs, firmly in the realms of Michael Crichton's science fiction novel. There are already very real self-assemblers all around us that owe nothing to nanotechnology. They are called viruses and bacteria. They pose a very real threat that is moreover increasing, due to our farming practices, profligate use of antibiotics and cheap international travel. The creation of this hazard obviously cannot be laid at the door of nanotechnology, although some of the nanoscale analysis techniques evolved for nanotechnology may well be able to held with combating it.

Concerns About Nanomaterials and Nanoparticles

What about the less spectacular aspects of nanotechnology? I have tried to show you earlier in the lecture how materials structured on the nanometer scale can give properties that are highly exploitable. Are there aspects of these materials that we need to be careful about? There is no doubt that the properties that give nanomaterials their technological exploitability might also give us cause for concern. We have already seen in the last 100 years how a single material with hugely beneficial properties can bring equally huge problems. Asbestos was very widely used in the period between the late 19th and mid-20th centuries. It has extraordinarily useful insulating properties. The high efficiency steam engines used in ocean-going liners and steam locomotives would have been impossible without it. However, we all now know how lethal a few asbestos fibres can be if inhaled, causing occupational cancers, and many people have died prematurely because of it. Is there any risk that any of the materials that are emerging from our nanotechnology labs might be building-up a similar problem for the future? There are certainly enough physical similarities between the dimensional characteristics of asbestos fibres and carbon nanotubes to cause some concern. At the moment we just don't know whether carbon nanotubes are hazardous; there has not been sufficient research. There has been a small amount of work in which rats inhaled carbon nanotubes, but the results were inconclusive. It is important to note that in all of the applications I have come across for carbon nanotubes, such as in composites or displays, the tubes would be very firmly fixed in a stable structure and would therefore be unlikely to pose a threat to the general public, although we should still ask questions about how the product would ultimately be disposed of. . . .

What about nanoparticles? Should we be concerned about inhaling these, or indeed rubbing them onto our skins? There is good evidence that we have been exposed to certain types of nanoparticles in the atmosphere for millennia. Wood-based campfires are excellent sources of nanoparticulate soot, for example. There is little cause for alarm in the sense that nanoparticles, *per se*, do not constitute a new hazard at low levels of exposure. However, there is good evidence that heavy exposure to carbon black is a serious industrial hazard, and that heavy exposure to nanoparticulate soot from sources such as diesel exhausts may be a cause of cancer. There is also evidence that, should nanoparticles arrive in the lungs, they do not remain there, but readily cross the barrier into the blood stream, whence they can migrate to various parts of the body, including the brain. There is, unfortunately, very little evidence to tell us what damage nanoparticles might cause there.

On the specific issue of sunscreens, it is known that the main oxides of interest are inert when present at the larger scale, but again there is a dearth of evidence about how the particles might behave when at the nanoscale. There is as yet, no evidence to suggest that they can penetrate into healthy skin, but the fact that nanoparticles are known to have different properties from those exhibited in the bulk must give us some cause for concern should they be ingested. There is a need for much more research in this area. . . .

Nanotechnology in the Defense Industry

Are there other areas for concern about nanotechnology? Nanotechnology, like virtually all technologies, is being considered for the contributions it can make to defence. These include obvious developments such as improved electronic systems for communications, improved sensors and, especially, improved materials. Examples include composites using carbon nanotubes and a novel body armour that uses oxide nanoparticles dispersed in a fluid and held between two flexible Kevlar sheets. The composite fabric is flexible, but any attempt to penetrate the sheets by, for example, a projectile or other weapon causes the fluid to rapidly set into a rigid mass that protects the wearer. The applications to flexible, wearable, protection that would protect a soldier's limbs as well as his torso are obvious. Metallic nanopowders can be expected to deliver more powerful conventional explosives. These developments would certainly give the armies using them a military edge, but hardly constitute the kind of doomsday scenario that we sometimes read about in the popular press or see on our video screens in movies like *Terminator II*. Those images owe more to science fiction based on the Drexler vision than a level-headed scientific analysis of the advances that nanotechnology is really likely to deliver.

Paradoxically, the broad contribution that nanotechnology can potentially make to economic development has sometimes been cited as a cause for concern, especially by some pressure groups. They point out that the promise of nanotechnology would widen the disparity in development between the rich and poor nations of the world. The rich will get richer, while the poor will be unable to benefit from the nanotechnology revolution. . . .

These questions of how we as a society choose to deploy or employ the capabilities that nanotechnology may provide are very good ones. But it strikes me that they are ethical issues that pertain more to the general capabilities that our modern technologies can deliver, rather than being specific issues concerning nanotechnology *per se*. They are, perhaps, more in the realm of the philosopher than the engineer. Nevertheless, the success of the nanotechnologists in promoting their area makes them natural targets for these ethical questions. We nanotechnologists need to make links with the people who can help us to answer them, and this is starting to happen. . . .

Nanotechnology Is a Useful Technology

I have tried to show how nanotechnology—the exploitation of matter when it is deliberately structured at the very small scale—has the potential to provide huge benefits, just as any useful technology should. It is a real, very broadly based and multidisciplinary area of human endeavour and not just a token epithet that can be applied to the latest research proposal or business venture in an attempt to get it funded, although admittedly it is frequently used that way. Certainly, there are issues that should concern us. These can be specific. We need, for example, to understand more about the health and environmental impacts of our uses of nanoparticles. There are also more general concerns. Nanotechnology could provide us with a broad range of capabilities but they need to be applied in a thoughtful and responsible manner. However, I would contend that these concerns are similar to those that might have been applied to any significant technology in the past. The only difference is that we are now in a position to learn from history and can try to take action before mistakes are made. I hope that I have made the case that the action should be both proportionate and based on a realistic analysis of the likely risks and benefits of nanotechnology.

| *"Nanotechnology seems to be a market-ing* branding *term, not a genuine and coherent research field."*

Nanotechnology Is Just a Marketing Term

Adolfo Gutierrez

In the following viewpoint, Adolfo Gutierrez argues that nano-technology hasn't, and won't, produce any valuable products, be-cause it is not a real field of science. According to Gutierrez, sci-entists do not define their work based on the dimensional scale in which they carry it out. For instance, he says, chemists call themselves organic chemists or inorganic chemists, not nanochem-ists or microchemists. Gutierrez thinks that the whole concept of nanotechnology is a marketing scheme, which may end up hav-ing many detrimental effects on researchers, investors, and entre-preneurs. Gutierrez has a PhD in Engineering Physics and is the director of uBricks Research in New York.

Alexander E. Braun and Adolfo Gutierrez, "The Nanotech Mirage—A Differing View," *Semiconductor International*, September 16, 2008. Copyright © 2009 Reed Business In-formation, a division of Reed Elsevier Inc. All rights reserved. Reproduced by permis-sion. www.semiconductor.net.

As you read, consider the following questions:

1. According to Gutierrez, defining a research field on dimension is an abstraction. What does he say defines the scientific nature of a research field?

2. What does Gutierrez say are three defocusing effects of defining a field based on dimensional scale?

3. According to Gutierrez, which company, IBM or Intel, does not refer to small electronics as "nanoelectronics?"

We seem to be stuck in the notion that nanotechnology is new science that opens new frontiers. However, nanotechnology seems to be a marketing *branding* term, not a genuine and coherent research field. Every physicist, chemist, biochemist, device engineer, materials engineer, etc., has dealt forever with small-scale science. This has been true since at least Aristotle's time. The notion that atoms can now be manipulated is also not new as evidenced, for example, by chemical synthesis. The only new thing is that we can now "observe" and "visualize" atoms better than before. Perhaps this visual experience is the real source of much of the past 10 years of nanomarketing excitement. Unfortunately, productive engineering at nanoscale is much more complex and costly than dramatic visualizations or physical probing; we are all painfully acknowledging this undeniable reality.

Dimensional Scale Is Not Important

I have pioneered several MEMS [microelectromechanical systems] and NEMS [nanoelectro mechanical systems] devices, and developed unique testing methods and instruments. In 1993, I originated the phrase, "Lab-on-a-Chip," started some businesses based on micro/nano technologies, and developed a few electron nanodevices; however, I've always been reluctant to brand these pursuits as "nanoscale" anything, as dimension *per se* is an abstraction with little meaning in the physical world. It is the manifestation of physical effects that defines the scientific nature of a research field.

Most traditional disciplines don't assign importance to the dimensional scale of the structures and processes involved; but only to functional outcomes—at any scale. For example, a researcher working in structures inside cells and microtubule transport processes has never called himself a nanobiologist; he's a functional microbiologist, a structural cell biologist or a biochemist. Likewise, no chemist would call himself an "atom nanoengineer," or a structural biologist a "life nanoengineer." They practice organic, inorganic, bio or structural chemistry based on functional outcomes, not dimensional scale.

Because language and reasoning are closely linked, the abuse of "nanoscale" as an all-encompassing word has had a distorting effect among scientists, policy makers, entrepreneurs and investors. This is important because young and inexperienced people are pursuing "nanocareers" in the hope that there will be a reward at the end of the formative "nanocycle," but there might be no career at all in a product, market and functionalities-driven world.

Nanotechnology, 10 years into the branded nano-era, has failed to deliver valuable products. Moreover, those involved in the field have resorted to wide-ranging definitions to include all kinds of functionally rich building blocks such as DNA bases, structural proteins, integrated sensors, logic gates, meta materials, and many other functional building blocks sharing dimensional scales but lacking relationships to functional effects.

Professionals of functionally defined fields are amused by this on-the-fly nano-marketers' redefinition of concepts. In fact, most of these now nano-concepts predate the nano-era and will, most likely, postdate it. The scientific and engineering challenges associated with these functional fields remain as challenging now as they were before the era of "nano branding."

Nano Definition: Too Broad and Too Narrow

But what makes a thing nanoscience? The easiest way to define the field is by the size of the objects being studied. The range given is one to one hundred nanometers, a size generally described as being one ten-thousandth the width of a human hair (the hair, like the state of Rhode Island, being one of our standard units of measurement). While simple and comprehensible, the size-based definition is considered both too broad and too narrow to be useful. It is too broad because it includes "passive" applications of the technology, like nanoscale particles used in cosmetics, sunscreens, and even clothing, as well as biological molecules like proteins and DNA. It is too narrow because the unique properties of nanoscale materials are not strictly limited to the specified sizes. But deciding on a better definition is troublesome, and researchers have yet to agree on one.

Daisy James, "Life In the Small Lane,"
Berkeley Science Review, *2008.*

Adverse Impacts of "Nano-branding"

The defocusing effects of defining a field based on scale are serious and can lead to research dilution, lack of synergies and poor-quality science. Imagine civil and device engineers, immunologists, physicians, and botanists defining themselves, their research fields as "meter-scale." How good would the resulting quality of those defocused efforts have been?

I see the adverse effects of nanoscale everything first-hand as a researcher, investor and entrepreneur in the "nanospace"; where nanotech has been so far one of the worst-performing scientific efforts in recent memory. After spending in excess of

$30 billion globally on R&D [research and development] since 1999, the world still awaits functional breakthroughs, products and payoffs. Naturally, funding is collapsing at a fast rate.

Delaying valuable outcomes under the forgiving mantle of "excessive difficulty" would be acceptable except that there's a long line of people waiting with their own non-nanobranded research agendas, and they're beginning to win policy battles, research dollars, and investors' confidence.

Intel and IBM Show Differing Approaches to Nanoelectronics

Boards are quickly abandoning their support for "nanoelectronics". Five of the main electronic companies have thrown in the towel since March of last year [2007], and investors have all but dried up nanoelectronics disbursements. National governments are slowing down funding and the field is retrenching the funding of structures that are difficult to qualify as objective or even competitive. Nanoelectronics research seems headed for a long and cold winter, deeply underfunded, clinging to fewer than five corporations worldwide, and a dozen surviving startups. Perhaps the business community is becoming increasingly uncomfortable with the very unclear risk vs. reward proposition offered by scientists and engineers.

Intel does not refer to small electronics as "nanoelectronics," it simply sees itself as developing awesome killer IT products for the next 100 years; in fact, the company discourages research under the mantle of "nanoelectronics." Interestingly enough, it's still a leader in nanoscale R&D.

IBM, on the other hand, is a big supporter of nanoelectronics. It regularly reports nano-breakthroughs, a most unexpected outcome as IBM as a relatively small R&D budget compared to the remaining integrated electronics industry. Regardless, IBM's real challenge is to convert its nano R&D into products that can contribute to the company's bottom line, as suggested by the recent Lucent-Alcatel decision. Up until about 18 months ago, Lucent-Alcatel used to report nano breakthroughs with an intensity similar to IBM's, but now they are being disbanded and their core research facility, Bell Labs, is officially out of integrated electronics basic and applied research, and their IC research lab has been shut down. They couldn't convert the results of their research into product lines fitting their remaining businesses. This is a lesson that should have a focusing effect on the few remaining players.

"Nano" Brand Will Eventually Lose Value

Once the "nano" brand losses its remaining value, will we once again focus our attention on functional outcomes and not on dimensional scale? This is a major issue, because we may well choose to focus R&D efforts on die stacking and complex packaging, advanced interconnects, parallel architectures and software optimization; and through that extend a functional version of Moore's Law [which describes the trend of technology to increase exponentially over time] that emphasizes end-to-end productivity gains, instead of steady miniaturization for its own sake.

Product focus always results in an efficient narrowing of options. Nano investments are delivering very little return because they are not bounded; they are spread very thinly across human knowledge. The Apollo Program put us on the moon by spending an amount comparable to that spent globally so far on nano research, over a similar period of time. The outcome was somewhat different because the goal was clear.

| "*[Nanotechnology] has considerable potential to be more Pandora's Box than Holy Grail.*"

Nanotechnology Concerns Currently Outweigh Any Potential Benefits

Michael Buerger

In the following viewpoint, Michael Buerger discusses what he thinks are future major societal threats from nanotechnology. In Buerger's future scenario, everyone, or everyone of a certain social class, has access to a "personal nanofactory," or molecular assembler, which can be used to make everything from toilet paper to drugs. Buerger posits that large corporations will try to control and earn profits from nanofactories. He also believes personal nanofactories could be used for criminal purposes, such as making illegal drugs or even to perpetrating mass murder. Eventually, Buerger believes that nanotechnologies will lead to social and religious upheaval. Buerger is an associate professor of criminal justice at Bowling Green State University and a former police officer.

As you read, consider the following questions:

1. What are the two ways that the dominant forces of the economy can maintain control over nanotechnology for monetary benefit, according to Buerger?

2. Buerger thinks that personal nanofactories could lead to widespread drug manufacturing analogous to what recent drug epidemic?

3. According to Buerger, a maturing nanotechnology could trigger social dislocation not seen since when?

On top of my physical desk sits a copy of *Pandaemonium: The Coming of the Machine as Seen by Contemporary Observers, 1660–1886.* Humphrey Jennings' "imaginative history of the Industrial Revolution." On my computer desktop are essays by the authors of this volume [*Nanotechnology Perceptions* volume 2], the possible precursors of *Pan-nano-daemonium: The Coming of the Micro-Machine.*

A Nano-Inspired "Englightment"—What Could Happen on Our Way There

In one of those essays, "The Need for Limits," Chris Phoenix speaks of the Enlightenment in terms of a synergy: enhanced human productivity with machines, partially supporting a philosophical examination of the human condition. Though certainly that, the Enlightenment also was a watershed period when the economic foundations of the European economy changed, and the authority of Revealed Truth was forced to contend with the authority of Rational Thought and its practical cousin, Scientific Inquiry. The shifts in the economy created a massive transformation of social life, from agrarian to urban. The current era has parallels to all of these forces, movements already in play but not yet complete . . . and in some cases not fully articulated.

As a peripheral member of a futurists group in my profes-sional field (policing, and more broadly, criminal justice), I have noticed that futurists tend to be concerned with the end results of trends, the state of things ten, twenty, or fifty years from now. By contrast, I am more concerned with the collat-eral damage we may sustain in the process of getting to those future states from where we are now.

This essay approaches that interstitial state in four sec-tions. The first section looks at the control of the technology; the second, for the criminal potentials inherent in it. Using the template of the Enlightenment, the third section looks at the darker channels of social transformation, particularly the impact on work and social worth. The fourth section draws an admittedly leap-of-faith parallel between the Enlighten-ment's impact on religious authority, and technology's impact upon the authority of economic capital and law.

Nanotechnology holds remarkable potential to change the world, but like most recent technologies, it emerges within a larger system of laws, codes of conduct, and social expecta-tions developed for previous capacities. Those mechanisms will shape its emerging uses, possibly retarding or constrain-ing the applications of the technology in undesirable ways. At issue is whether micro-level processing will be merely one more tool (and thus alter our lives incrementally), or a Promethean[1] breakthrough that will alter human existence in profound ways. My interest, as one who stands outside the Halls of Science looking in, tends to center on the possibilities that I can understand from a layman's perspective.

Trying to grasp in layman's terms the implications of a new and only marginally understood technology leads to a search for analogies, framing the new in terms of the familiar (for good or ill).

---

1. In Greek mythology Prometheus was a Titan who stole fire from the God Olympus and gave it to mankind. To be Promethean is to be bold, inspiring, and creative.

Who Would Control Personal Nanofactories?

As a non-scientist, the most salient question for me is, "When do I get to play with the new toy?" Given the general limits of corporate use of nanotechnology, the first new toy that will become available to me most likely will be the desktop assembler, or personal nanofactory (PN).

The most knowledgeable members of CRN's [the Center for Responsible Nanotechnology's] Global Task Force have engaged in a lengthy discussion about desktop manufacturing and its social consequences, and as of this writing, there seems to be a lack of consensus about the capacity, and thus the full impact, of PNs. If we accept the position of the optimists, and expect fully capable devices to be available in the not-too-distant future, secondary questions arise: Will the devices be provided in fully capable form (probably transformative), or will their functionality be curtailed in defense of the corporate profits to be derived from them? If the latter, how will control be maintained? Some answers are perhaps to be found in current trends, since the courts often look to historical analogs in dealing with new issues.

If we posit that desktop manufacturing becomes widely available, as seems inevitable, the dominant forces of the economy have two avenues of recourse to maintain control over the new technology for monetary benefit. The first will be the control of raw materials for molecular assembly, which appears to share the delivery profile of heating fuels in contemporary life. More important is the second area, already suggested by Phoenix: patents and copyrights.

Patents and Copyrights

The development of nanotechnology is taking place within a corporate nest of ideas and resources (much like licensed computer software development), with some independent researchers and consortia operating on a freeware basis. Molecular assembly at any sort of commercial or individual level will require patterns to guide assembly, and these are likely to be controlled by patents. The majority of patents are almost certain to be controlled by corporate interests. Renewable user site licenses, comparable to commercial software packages, are the most likely form of retaining economic benefit for a corporate entity. One of the possible ways of maintaining economic control over site licenses would be some form of cyber-degradable program that self-destructs after a finite period, and must be renewed. For example, a user could download (or purchase on a one-use or renewable-use media platform) the code that would allow the manufacture of only a certain number of rolls of toilet paper by a personal nanofactory.

Patents and the fundamental premises of intellectual property are already under challenge, but the challenges have been met with an equally strong legal response anchored in precedent. The courts have handed the reins of control over digital recordings of music to the star-making machinery behind the popular songs through conservative interpretation of intellectual property statutes. The huge profits to be made from licensing technological advancements for industry virtually assures that the field of nanotechnology will be similarly bound.

The most recent Promethean technology, file-sharing, theoretically stood to liberate music from the chains of capital. However, Napster, Kaaza, Grokster, and their lesser clones have lost the legal battles, and the technology has been co-opted by industry giants into new distribution-for-profit mechanisms. Corporations and universities alike write eminent domain over patents and patentable discoveries into their employment contracts, and genetic patterns and discoveries are subject to copyright. Unknown garage bands and the metaphorical garage workshops of independent researchers still can be found beyond the current reach of over-grasping capital, but only until they become good or useful enough to attract attention. . . .

While the first generation of personal nanofactories probably will come with a fixed number of pre-programmed patterns, market forces will demand versatility. Units will need a capacity to acquire new assembly patterns as they are developed, and there seem to be few options beyond what is now available for computer data. Patterns may be downloaded over hardwired or Wi-Fi networks, or be manually transferred by whatever media replace the current disk drives and flash memory sticks. Each format would spawn a black market of unknown proportions, and with the black markets come the accompanying risks of epidemic and pandemic consequences of criminal use.

Personal Nanofactories Used for Criminal Intent

We should anticipate that a new drug industry will piggyback on the basic molecular assembly phenomenon, and the potential implications for the social fabric are enormous. One of the most desirable benefits of nanotechnology is that of precise targeting of therapeutic drugs; however, the same technology will have associated benefits for illegal pharmacopoeia. While the complexity of the patterns most likely will delay this until a second or third-level level of PN development, once the basic patterns for psychotropic drugs are understood and the assembly technology sufficiently enabled, individual drug manufacture is almost certain to become a social tsunami. There are strong analogies to the current methamphetamine epidemic: less than two decades ago, the manufacture of crystal methamphetamine required a well-equipped clandestine lab, a chemist, a criminal organization for protection and distribution. Today, meth is the new bathtub gin, easily made in any number of Rube Goldberg[2] processes in basements, trailers, campers, garages, or pickup trucks.

2. Rube Goldberg was a political cartoonist whose cartoons depicted complex machines that performed simple tasks.

Unlike methamphetamine, a micro-assembly drug manufacture process would need only the basic molecular components, not the more elaborate precursor chemicals (like pseudoephedrine) whose control is now part of our anti-drug strategy. That suggests a much greater availability, with corollary hazards of greater social experimentation and conceivably even poly-drug experimentation. The toxic byproducts of meth labs are threats to law enforcement agencies, the families of meth addicts, and neighborhoods. We do not yet know the degree to which micro-manufacture byproducts will be toxic, if at all.

Illicit micro-manufacture may be a mixed blessing. On the one hand, effectively eliminating organized crime from the market may lessen the toxic effects of the war on drugs: the corruption involved with importation of drugs, and the violence of competing drug markets. At least potentially, even the criminogenic nature of drug dependency may be lessened: since the base materials would likely be the same as for legitimate micro-manufacture, it is less likely that a specialized, higher-priced supply chain would be necessary. The dynamics of that supply chain create additional crimes: violence among criminal enterprises competing for turf high, and both personal and property crime committed by addicts desperate to meet the dealer's price. Absent the supply market, the cost of personally manufactured drugs would be cheaper, and the risks of their creation considerably lower in terms of legal discovery and interdiction. However, the potential free access to addictive and mind-altering substances will almost certainly exacerbate the social problems associated with the addictions and dependencies that result. The same delivery method could surreptitiously create markets for new designer drugs, addictive and involuntarily piggybacked on legitimately disseminated nanoproduct codes. The number of "what ifs" that need to be resolved before either scenario happens leave the possi-

Nanofactory Basics

The nanofactory system described here incorporates a large number of fabricators under computer control. In a single *product cycle*, each fabricator produces one *nanoblock*, approximately the same size as the fabricator. The blocks are then joined together, eight sun-blocks making one block twice as big. This process is repeated until eight large blocks are produced, and finally joined in an arrangement that is not necessarily cubical. The output of multiple product cycles may be combined to produce large products. The production system is arranged in a three-dimensional hierarchical branching structure, which allows the sub-block assembly to be done by machinery of appropriate size. Eight factories of a given size can be combined to form one larger factory; the 64 blocks produced are joined into eight blocks twice as big. The design is easily scalable to tabletop size, with a ~ 1 meter factory producing eight ~ 5 cm blocks per product cycle. . . . The blocks need not be solid cubes, and their interior may be quite complex. . . . Products can be unfolded after manufacture, greatly increasing the range of possible product structures and allowing products to be much larger than the nanofactory that produced them.

Chris Phoenix, "Design of a Primitive Nanofactory,"
Journal of Evolution and Technology, *October 2003.*

bilities within the realm of fiction for now, but if the analogies to the Internet hold true, they must be anticipated as a contingency. . . .

Mass Murder Via Personal Nanofactories

Downstream, there is also the potential for mass murder via compromised assembly codes. In the physical world, tainting a medicine with poison can only be done efficiently at the factory source, and even then must bypass or defeat stringent quality control measures. Any other corruption can take place only on a relatively small scale. The introduction of a virulent and unsuspected corruption of a drug assembly code is not so limited. It shares more in common with the computer virus than the Tylenol poisoner [seven people died in 1982 after taking Tylenol that had been laced with potassium cyanide]. Since black market codes originate and enter the data stream outside the domain of legitimate quality control measures, and the drug-using community is unlikely to give designer drug codes great scrutiny (at least in the initial rounds), "massassination" (mass assassination or "pharmaceutical cleansing") via bogus codes is a distinct possibility in a networked distribution system. It would challenge both medical institutions and law enforcement agents. It is admittedly an outside possibility, requiring a rare combination of technological savvy and social alienation, but the world since September 2001 has been dealing with more and more "one in a bazillion" scenarios. Nothing should be taken off the table in terms of exploring, and preparing for, unpleasant misappropriation of technology. . . .

Defenses to such a scenario potentially exist, but security measures are one of the most attractive fruits of the Tree of Knowledge. Like contemporary Internet defenses, and the laws passed to outlaw new designer drugs, defensive maneuvers almost always stimulate new offensive attacks. Any combination of zeros and ones, in any transportation medium, can be hijacked and compromised: the track record of Internet security does not bode well for the free and easy commercial transfer of assembly codes for the molecules-up creation of products.

Personal Nanofactories Could Lead to Massive Job Loss

During the Industrial Revolution in England, improved agricultural efficiencies accelerated the process of enclosure, dislocating the rural population no longer needed for raising and harvesting crops. Simultaneous improvements in the production of iron and steel, in weaving, and other areas began to transform cottage industries into factory-based industries, and urbanization rapidly changed the face of the country. The nature of trade shifted from one-off mercantile ventures and royal charters to stable capital for long-term ventures. Factory industries supplanted cottage industries, local artisans, and craft guilds, but the concentration of work in brick-and-mortar containers still left some out of work: the notorious "surplus labor" that kept wages low. The expansion of the new manufacturing base managed to absorb surplus labor for some time, until the advent of widespread robotics in the second half of the twentieth century.

A robust generation of personal nanofactories may very well bifurcate [divide] commerce into those items that can be manufactured at home and those which still must be purchased through the familiar retail supply chains. While a certain amount of jobs will be created around the transportation of raw materials for PNs, they will be paltry in comparison to the jobs the devices displace in manufacture, transport, and sales. Globalization has already imposed a certain amount of social dislocation in the manufacturing sectors; a maturing nanotechnology could very well trigger a long-term social dislocation not seen since the English migration from the newly-enclosed farmlands to the new factories of the Industrial Revolution. . . .

Social Marginalization

Another of the volumes on my physical desktop is William Julius Wilson's *When Work Disappears: The World of the New Urban Poor*. It deals with the "left behind" problem of those under a double burden of low social status and of being dependent upon jobs in industries that have moved elsewhere (to Alabama, to Mexico, or to China). While the analogy to a nanotechnology shift need not be exact, Wilson's depictions and analyses offer a powerful warning we may need to confront within a generation: what are the social consequences when there are no alternative employment outlets for surplus labor? American history of the 20th century holds small hope that our social attitudes will change rapidly: the unemployed, underemployed, and "idle" always have been despised for not somehow rising above the crushing weight of social and economic forces beyond their control. Revolution traditionally has been pointless or counterproductive, and Cite Soliel [an area of extreme poverty in Haiti] endures in its multiple forms around the globe despite the potential and promises of globalization, the Green Revolution, and countless other advances. . . .

Larger questions arise out of this potential for increased social marginality. The income gap between rich and poor has been widening for more than two decades. Globalization has transformed the American economy, and the household economy has suffered as a result. The degree to which nanotechnology, the Internet, and other technologies accelerate or buffer the social decoupling of work and status is still an undiscovered country. If the cumulative effect is acceleration, we need to anticipate the range of human adaptations that will follow. If one no longer is attached in any meaningful way to an economy and the political ideology that supports it, how long can that authority hold one's allegiance? And what are the alternatives if the allegiance cannot otherwise be reinforced?

Nanotechnology's Impact on Religious Authority

Although it is a commonplace to think of religious worship as timeless, it actually undergoes periodic major shifts, often triggered by secular events. In the first century of the Common Era, the nature of revelation itself was transformed from the direct presence of a transcendent deity to the interpretation of a written Scripture. For Jews, the destruction of the Holy of Holies in the Second Temple ended the traditional direct contact of the High Priests. For Christians, the sudden absence of their Messiah from the streets of Jerusalem transformed the Judaic concept of messianic return into an entirely new understanding [of] the relationship between human beings and their Creator.

The struggle for primacy between the Catholic Church and secular governments began soon after Christianity was adopted as the official religion of the Roman Empire. It continued through the Investiture Controversy of the Middle Ages, and was the decisive factor in the success of the Reformation. However, the waning of the dominance of religion was a process begun centuries earlier by resistance ("heresy") within the Church itself, beginning with the Great Schism of the Eastern Orthodox traditions. The purification movements that created monastic orders within the Church presaged the later coming of the Reformation, which relocated purifying reform outside the Church and ended the sole authority of Rome to arbitrate Christian salvation. The secular challenges arising from the Enlightenment remain at play in the contemporary questions of Church and State, Science and Belief, and authority to define human relations. Increasing secularity jousts with the rise of fundamentalism and of sects, undermining traditional "mainstream" churches.

Whether the maturing of nanotechnology will impact the continuing struggle of religious authority is unclear. The potential is there, certainly, as the manipulation of matter at the molecular level comes perilously close to "playing God," especially where it might affect what it means to be human. Artificial intelligence, genetic engineering, and cybernetic enhancements pose imminent challenges to the religious understandings of "human," and nanotechnology bids to play a major role within each of those technologies. Public discourse in areas where the definitions of "life" are most con-tended are fueled as much by symbolism and metaphor as by science; misapprehensions and misunderstandings about nano-technology may well be fuel for new battlefronts in what has been dubbed "the culture wars.". . .

More Pandora's Box than Holy Grail

Nanotechnology has its own limits. A host of major decisions in the social realm will not be changed to any great degree by nanotechnology. It will not protect the Arctic Natural Wildlife Refuge (indeed, if natural gas is the first and basic fuel for desktop manufacturing, it may exacerbate the pressures on the ANWR), nor will it stop the denuding of the Amazon rain forest. It will not eliminate prejudice, nor resolve the multiple questions of authority and Authority that attend the modern estate of humankind. We can predict safely that when this particular future of mature nanotechnology arrives, it will not be equally distributed, and may easily be a weapon of social dominance rather than the delivery vehicle of social equity. Even the utopian visions of Gene Roddenberry [creator of Star Trek] included a period of troubled dystopia, which Alvin Toffler captured in *Future Shock*: "the premature arrival of the future . . . the imposition of a new culture on an old one" that results in "human beings . . . increasingly disoriented, progres-sively incompetent to deal with their environments."

Which leaves me almost where I began: What do I make of this nanotechnology thing? I suspect it will be very much like its predecessors, a potentially transformative technology that will be bound on the bed of Procrustes[3] of the older so-cial and economic systems that midwifed it. Because of that, it has considerable potential to be more Pandora's Box than Holy Grail in the early going. Assuming that its byproducts do

3. In Greek mythology Procrustes had an iron bed that he invited passersby to lie down in. Those too tall were amputated. Those too short were stretched. Nobody ever fit into the bed because it was secretly adjustable. A Procrustean bed refers to forced confor-mity.

not poison the groundwater or become an airborne grey goo, it will almost have to achieve an outlaw status (or its more egalitarian potential championed by those who will be deemed outlaws) before it reaches a socially transformative cusp. In the near term, whether I buy it in a store or make it with my nanofactory, I will still have to pay for toilet paper.

| "Some of the grandest ideas about how to preserve the environment involve molecular-scale engineering known as nanotechnology."

Nanotechnology Can Benefit the Environment

Barnaby J. Feder

In the following viewpoint, Barnaby J. Feder contends that nanotechnology can benefit the environment, however, most people aren't aware of nanotechnology's "greenness." He says nanotechnology's most promising green offerings include window coatings that keep buildings warm and reduce the need for air conditioning, as well as light-emitting-diodes that can replace inefficient incandescent lightbulbs. Nanocatalysts can reduce industrial waste and energy consumption, while nanoparticles can clean up contaminated waste sites. According to Feder, despite nanotechnology's potential to help the environment, some environmentalists remain worried about the long-term impact of nanotechnology. Feder has been a New York Times *technology reporter since 1980.*

As you read, consider the following questions:

1. According to Feder, to most Americans nanotechnology means what?

2. According to Feder, new nanotechnology coatings for windows cut infrared penetration by what percentage?

3. According to Feder, nanoscale particles composed of what metallic compound can help clean up soil contaminated with PCBs and dry cleaning fluids?

Some of the grandest ideas about how to preserve the environment involve molecular-scale engineering known as nanotechnology. Such visions might inspire more confidence, though, if there were real products available to achieve them.

Nanotechnology's supporters have been talking for more than a decade about fashioning new metals, plastics and biological compounds that could enable innovations like increasingly efficient batteries for electric cars and solar energy panels for homes. They also say that nanotechnology can be used to restore damaged environments—by cleansing polluted soil, for example, with tiny particles that could make toxins harmless.

There is nothing implausible about such ideas. It is easy to see how the ability to manipulate matter at the scale of a few nanometers, or billionths of a meter, could lead to environmental breakthroughs. That is one reason billions of dollars are being spent on nanotechnology research.

Nanotechnology's Greenness Not Yet Apparent

For now, though, nanotechnology is often linked to the environment in a negative way: the fear of the potential hazards posed by novel inventions. Novelists like Michael Crichton have imagined nanoscale robots creating an ecodisaster. On a more practical level, toxicologists are struggling to assess the damage actual particles can do to living cells and laboratory animals.

Unfortunately for nanotechnology's reputation, the most exciting green nanoproducts are still on the drawing boards. To most Americans, nanotechnology means limited improvements, as in stain-resistant clothing, super durable bowling balls or transparent sunscreens.

"The first products the public has heard about have been luxury items," said David M. Berube, a professor of communications at the University of South Carolina, who studies public perception of nanotechnology. The next highly visible wave will include antibacterial cleaning agents, followed by pharmaceuticals and medical devices, he said.

But the absence of a symbolic green nanotech product does not mean there is no progress. "While shifts to cleaner and greener sources of energy are critical, energy conservation remains the most powerful lever to improve the environment," said Sean Murdock, executive director of the Nano-Business Alliance, a trade group. And nanotechnology has been playing a role in energy conservation for decades.

Nano-Coated Windows That Cut Energy Demand

Mr. Murdock said the best example might be specialized glass for commercial buildings that PPG Industries began marketing in 1982. A transparent coating only a few nanometers thick sharply increased buildings' ability to retain heat. That cut their demand for energy.

Since then, PPG has developed a far more environmentally beneficial window named Solarban, which slashes demand for air-conditioning in warm climates. The trick has been to develop transparent coatings that block light at infrared frequencies, which add heat. The new coatings cut infrared penetration by 46 percent while allowing more light to get through than earlier, less-effective infrared-reflecting windows.

Environmental Benefits of Nanotechnology

As applications of nanotechnology develop over time, they have the potential to help shrink the human footprint on the environment. This is important, because over the next 50 years the world's population is expected to grow 50%, global economic activity is expected to grow 500%, and global energy and materials use is expected to grow 300%. So far, increased levels of production and consumption have offset our gains in cleaner and more-efficient technologies. This has been true for municipal waste generation, as well as for environmental impacts associated with vehicle travel, groundwater pollution, and agricultural runoff. . . . Nanotechnology can create materials and products that will not only directly advance our ability to detect, monitor, and clean up environmental contaminants, but also help us avoid creating pollution in the first place.

U.S. Environmental Protection Agency,
Nanotechnology White Paper, *February 2007.*

But PPG's Solarban windows and similar products are—and will probably remain—too costly for most homeowners or for commercial buildings. So some experts say that a better example of the environmental benefits of nanotechnology may be the light-emitting diode [L.E.D.].

L.E.D.'s and Catalysts

L.E.D.'s have already replaced old-fashioned incandescent bulbs in traffic lights. Now, because of improvements in the light-emitting microchips, white L.E.D.'s show signs of becoming an alternative to fluorescent lights as a replacement for the staggeringly inefficient but cheap incandescent bulb in other uses.

"When you go to Japan, they don't even use incandescent Christmas tree lights anymore," said Stephen B. Maebius, a patent lawyer in the nanotechnology field. "It's all white L.E.D.'s."

Less noticeable to consumers are advances in catalysts, said Barbara Karn, a nanotechnology expert in the research arm of the Environmental Protection Agency. Nanotechnologists have been successfully tinkering with the metals and other materials used as catalysts at oil refineries or in automotive catalytic converters. They are exploiting basic science: the smaller the particles of a catalyst can be made, the more surface area is available to assist reactions. That leads to faster chemical reactions, energy savings and less waste.

There could be a downside, Ms. Karn said. Some of the industrial products benefiting from the nanocatalysts are toxic chemicals. Making them cleaner and cheaper to produce may leave the industry with less incentive to find safer alternatives.

Cleaning Up Waste Sites

Ms. Karn said a different symbol of green nanotechnology might be the products being synthesized to clean up waste sites, especially nanoscale particles of iron compounds that have been under development since the mid-1990s. When injected into contaminated soil, they have proved far more effective than larger iron-based compounds at breaking down hazardous organic compounds like PCBs and dry-cleaning fluids, and at neutralizing poisons like lead and arsenic.

Six ounces of nanoscale particles does the job of a ton of micron-size particles because of their vastly increased surface area and the greater ease with which they move through the soil in water, said Wei-xian Zhang, a pioneer in the field at Lehigh University in Bethlehem, Pa.

Environmentalists Still Leery

Environmentalists say they remain worried about the long-term impact of dumping novel nanomaterials into the environment to clean up hazardous wastes. And there is another potential downside. Jennifer Sass, the senior scientist at the Natural Resources Defense Council, said that any nanotechnology cleanup product could deflect attention from the underlying problem.

"I hope the public will ask probing questions like, 'Who put that pollution there in the first place, and why didn't the government stop them?'" she said.

"It is a matter of concern that we were repeatedly told by competent organisations and individuals that there is currently insufficient information to form a definitive judgement about the safety of many types of nanomaterials."

Nanotechnology's Health and Environmental Impacts Are Unknown

Royal Commission on Environmental Pollution

In the following viewpoint, the British Royal Commission on Environmental Pollution contends that there is a complete lack of scientific data about the health and environmental impacts of nanoparticles, despite indications these particles pose significant risks. In order to assess the challenges and benefits associated with nanotechnology, the Royal Commission reviewed scientific literature and questioned organizations and individuals in the nanotechnology industry. They concluded that there is reason for concern about nanoparticles' environmental and health impacts. These particles have potential to enter the environment and cer-

Royal Commission on Environmental Pollution Contributors, "Summary," *Novel Materials in the Environment: The Case of Nanotechnology,* Summary Report, Norwich, U.K.: Royal Commission on Environmental Pollution, 2008. Copyright © 2008 Crown. Reproduced by permission. www.rcep.org.uk.

tain kinds of nanoparticles, such as nanotubes and nanosilver particles, can be toxic. The Royal Commission calls for more research into the health and environmental risks of nanoparticles. The Royal Commission on Environmental Pollution is an independent body, appointed by the Queen of England, which publishes in-depth reports on what it identifies as the crucial environmental issues facing the United Kingdom and the world.

As you read, consider the following questions:

1. What class of nanomaterial has potential applications in lubricants and electrical conductors? What does the Royal Commission say is perhaps the best known example of this class of nanomaterial?

2. According to the Royal Commission, how long could it take for a new toxicological or ecotoxicological testing procedure to achieve regulatory acceptance?

3. What kinds of nanomaterials does the Royal Commission say are likely to present the most immediate toxicological hazard to living organisms and why?

The small size of nanomaterials gives them specific or enhanced physico-chemical properties, compared with the same materials at the macroscale. This results in great interest in their potential for development for different uses and products. A good working definition of a nanomaterial is one that is between 1 and 100 nm [nanometers] in at least one dimension.

Nanomaterials can have one, two or three dimensions in the nanoscale. One-dimensional nanomaterials include layers, multi-layers, thin films, platelets and surface coatings. They have been developed and used for decades, particularly in the electronics industry. Materials that are nanoscale in two dimensions include nanowires, nanofibres made from a variety of elements other than carbon, nanotubes and, a subset of this group, carbon nanotubes.

Materials that are nanoscale in three dimensions are known as nanoparticles. They exist naturally (for example, natural ammonium sulphate particles), but they can also be manufactured, as for example in the case of metal oxides such as titanium dioxide and zinc oxide. Metal oxide nanoparticles already have applications in cosmetics, textiles and paints and, in the longer term, could potentially be used for targeted drug delivery. Buckminsterfullerenes (also known as fullerenes and Buckyballs) are a class of nanomaterial of which carbon-60 (C_{60}) is perhaps the best known. Potential applications include use as lubricants and electrical conductors. . . .

Nanoparticles Have Unique Properties

The properties and functionalities of nanomaterials can be very different from those of the bulk form. Furthermore, some properties being discovered have not previously been observed in traditional chemistry or materials science. While the resulting difference in behaviour from the bulk form makes it possible to use nanomaterials in novel ways, it may also give rise to different mobility and toxicity in organisms and the environment.

The features of nanoparticles which underlie these properties and behaviour include: greatly increased surface area per unit mass; changes in surface reactivity and charge; and modified electronic characteristics. The electronic features can become quantized, leading to so-called 'quantum effects' which can influence optical, electrical, magnetic and catalytic behaviour. The strong surface forces which may be exhibited at this size range are also important as they may play a significant role in self-assembly of nanostructures.

It follows that some novel properties of nanoparticles are predictable, but others will be unexpected. These effects are often well characterised in relation to the functionalities for which the new properties are being exploited. However, they are usually much less well characterised in terms of fate and behaviour in organisms and the environment, or not characterised at all.

While the basic principles employed in characterising substances for health and environmental effects are the same whether or not they are in the nanoform, certain properties are particularly or uniquely important in the case of nanomaterials. These include particle size, particle shape, surface properties, solubility, agglomeration and aggregation. Furthermore, the way these properties determine behaviour can be profoundly influenced by extrinsic variables, such as temperature, pH, ionic strength of containing medium and presence or absence of light.

The Health and Environmental Impacts of Nanoparticles Are Unknown

It is a matter of concern that we were repeatedly told by competent organisations and individuals that there is currently insufficient information to form a definitive judgement about the safety of many types of nanomaterials. In some cases, the methods and data needed to understand the toxicology and exposure routes of nanomaterials are insufficiently standardised or even absent. There appears to be no clear consensus among scientists about how to address this deficit.

Current toxicological protocols for general chemical substances are fairly coarse screening mechanisms which tend to pick up acute effects. Almost by definition, with novel materials and particularly nanomaterials, there are virtually no data on chronic, long-term effects on people, other organisms or the wider environment.

So, new toxicological and ecotoxicological testing protocols are required. However, and crucially, under current procedures, it can take up to 15 years for a new testing protocol to achieve regulatory acceptance. Given the rapid pace of market penetration of nanomaterials and the products that contain

Greenpeace Calls for a Moratorium

In the absence of any established regulatory system, Greenpeace is calling for an immediate moratorium on the release of nanotechnological materials and products.

Greenpeace recommends the development of comprehensive national and/or international regulation that specifically addresses issues of nanotoxicity as well as the broader social and ethical issues related to the research, manufacture, consumption and environmental release of nanotechnological products.

Greenpeace, Nanotechnology Policy and Position Paper, *February 26, 2007.*

them, existing regulatory approaches cannot be relied upon to even detect, let alone manage, problems before a material has become ubiquitous [seemingly everywhere].

Difficulties also arise because the form in which materials make their way into the environment might not be the same as that encountered during manufacture. Many free nanoparticles agglomerate and aggregate in the natural environment, forming larger structures that may have different toxicological properties to those exhibited by the original nanoform.

Most nanomaterials are incorporated into products whose specific behaviour and properties are often well understood, but our inquiries suggested that very little thought has been given to their environmental impact as they become detached from products in use or at the point of final disposal. Moreover, techniques for their routine monitoring in the environment are not widely available, nor is it currently possible to determine their persistence in the environment or their transformation into other forms. Laboratory assessments of toxicity suggest that some nanomaterials could give rise to biological damage. But to date, adverse effects on populations or communities of organisms *in situ* ["in place"] have not been investigated and potential effects on ecosystem structure and processes have not been addressed. Ignorance of these matters brings into question the level of confidence that can be placed in current regulatory arrangements.

Nanoparticles Have Multiple Pathways into the Environment

As nanomaterials become incorporated into more and more consumer and industrial products, the routes by which they might enter organisms and the environment rapidly increases. They may be discharged directly into rivers or the atmosphere by industry, or inadvertently escape when products are used or disposed of in the environment, for example paints, cosmetics, sunscreens and pharmaceuticals.

In view of the apparent absence of evidence of harmful impacts of manufactured nanomaterials in 'real world' situations, we can only examine the plausibility of damage based on the extrapolation of evidence from laboratory investigations and occupational exposure studies on dust and other related substances. As is often the case in toxicology, the approach which remains is to identify the characteristics of the manufactured nanomaterial in question, determine its bioavailability and persistence in natural settings, then use data derived from measured or estimated concentrations in the environment as well as toxicological research in the laboratory to assess potential hazards and risks. However, although there is a widespread consensus that comprehensive characterisation of nanomaterials, during manufacture, use and disposal, is required to understand fully their potential fate and effects on human health and the environment, such characterisation is lacking in the vast majority of studies. . . .

More Ignorance About Nanoparticle Toxicology

Free manufactured nanoparticles and nanotubes (e.g. powders) are likely to present the most immediate toxicological hazard to living organisms as they are at liberty to interact with organisms in the wider environment. There is not the same level of concern regarding fixed nanomaterials (i.e. those incorporated into solid matrices or attached to surfaces), although there is clearly potential for them to become detached and enter natural ecosystems, especially when products containing them abrade [wear down] or weather during use or when they are disposed of as waste or are recycled.

Evidence presented to us on the environmental and human health risks posed by nanomaterials has often been contradictory. On the one hand some environmental scientists and policy makers feel strongly that the threat posed by most nanomaterials is small, whereas others are clearly worried about the possible toxicity of some nanomaterials, both to the wider environment and to human health. For example, concern was expressed about an increased risk of lung and cardiovascular damage from carbon nanotubes and C60 in humans, and the effects of nanosilver particles on microbial communities and sediment-feeding organisms. There is a consensus that mechanisms of toxicity are poorly understood and that, with minor exceptions, appropriate ecological studies have not been undertaken, including studies that address food chain transfer and multi-generational effects. Currently it is extremely difficult to evaluate how safe or how dangerous some nanomaterials are because of our complete ignorance about so many aspects of their fate and toxicology.

From an extensive review of the original published literature, several important conclusions can be drawn:

- There appears to be little consensus over the critical or even most important characteristics of manufactured nanomaterials that determine their toxicity profiles.

- Little information is available on how the various physical and chemical properties interact to generate an overall toxicity profile for a particular nanomaterial.

- There has been little attempt to use standard particles to study individual characteristics and their interactions, nor concerted attempts to develop approaches similar to quantitative structure-activity relationships (QSARs) that are currently being used for traditional chemicals.

- Knowledge on the medical applications of nanomaterials with respect to organ, cell and sub-cellular localisation should be harnessed to aid understanding of predictive toxicology.

The number of experimental centres involved in nanotoxicology is small and they seem to use different materials and experimental protocols. There is an urgent need for standardisation and co-ordination of research effort and focus in this field, although we are aware of, and welcome, the efforts being made to address these problems through the Organisation for Economic Co-operation and Development (OECD). There is also remarkably little link between knowledge gained from ecotoxicology and that from the study of toxicity in higher organisms including humans. Greater co-ordination and application of basic principles is needed between the two fields of research.

Toxicology Research Is Urgently Needed

Toxicology as a discipline has declined over the last 20 years in the UK [United Kingdom], Europe and the US [United States] with reduced training and career development dedicated to this subject. The requirement for high quality science, the integration needed between the biological and physical sciences and the urgent need for scientists to integrate findings from animal toxicology and ecotoxicology demands that more attention is given to toxicology training in our higher education institutions to take on the challenges of nanotoxicology.

In principle, all these issues can be addressed by more research. But the Commission is very concerned by the long lead times required for research to provide results that will be useful for legislation and regulation. We received expert opinion that lead times of 'several decades' could easily be involved. As a consequence, and however good the research effort, significant uncertainties and areas of ignorance will remain.

> "Nanotechnology could soon be applied to address the critical health, food, water, and energy needs of the 5 billion people in the developing world."

Nanotechnology Can Improve Global Equity

Peter Singer, Fabio Salamanca-Buentello, and Abdallah S. Daar

In the following viewpoint, Peter Singer, Fabio Salamanca-Buentello, and Abdallah Daar maintain that nanotechnology can be harnessed to help the poor and reduce global inequities. The authors queried a panel of international experts to come up with a list of ten ways nanotechnology can help developing nations. Most experts think that applying nanotechnology to energy production, agricultural productivity, and water treatment can help developing nations the most. According to the authors, developing countries, such as India, Brazil, and China must take the lead to foster nanotechnology research in these areas. The authors believe, however, it is a moral imperative that the global community assist developing countries in their nanotechnology endeavors. With effort on all parts, the authors believe that nanotechnology can be used to reduce the divide between rich countries and poor countries. Singer is the director of the University of Toronto Joint Centre for Bioethics, and along with Daar, he is co-director of the Canadian Program in Genomics and Global Health. Salamanca-Buentello is a researcher in nanotechnology.

As you read, consider the following questions:

1. What factors were the international panel of experts asked to consider when ranking the applications of nanotechnology most likely to benefit less industrialized nations?

2. According to the authors, what fraction of the world's population lacks access to safe water?

3. According to the authors, what percentage of funding did Canadian Prime Minister Martin propose should be used to help address the challenges faced by developing countries?

Developing countries usually find themselves on the sidelines watching the excitement of technological innovation. The wealthy industrialized nations typically dominate the development, production, and use of new technologies. But many developing countries are poised to rewrite the script in nanotechnology. They see the potential for nanotechnology to meet several needs of particular value to the developing world and seek a leading role for themselves in the development, use, and marketing of these technologies. As the next major technology wave, nanotechnology will be revolutionary in a social and economic as well as a scientific and technological sense.

Developing Countries Developing Their Own Nanotechnology

Developing countries are already aware that nanotechnology can be applied to many of their pressing problems, and they realize that the industrialized countries will not place these applications at the top of their to-do list. The only way to be certain that their needs are addressed is for less industrialized nations themselves to take the lead in developing those applications. In fact, many of these countries have already begun to do so. The wealthy nations should see this activity as a potential catalyst for the type of innovative research and economic development sorely needed in these countries. Strategic help from the developed world could have a powerful impact on the success of this effort. Planning this assistance should begin with an understanding of developing-country technology needs and knowledge of the impressive R&D [research and development] efforts that are already under way.

To provide strategic focus to nanotechnology efforts, we recently carried out a study using a modified version of the Delphi method[1] and worked with a panel of 63 international experts, 60 percent of whom were from developing countries, to identify and rank the 10 applications of nanotechnology most likely to benefit the less industrialized nations in the next 10 years. The panelists were asked to consider impact, burden, appropriateness, feasibility, knowledge gaps, and indirect benefits of each application proposed. Our results, [in the following list] show a high degree of consensus with regard to the top four applications: All of the panelists cited at least one of the top four applications in their personal top-four rankings, with the majority citing at least three.

Top 10 Applications of Nanotechnology for Developing Countries:

1. Energy storage, production, and conversion

2. Agricultural productivity enhancement

3. Water treatment and remediation

4. Disease diagnosis and screening

1. The Delphi Method is a method used to forecast or predict the future using input from an international panel of experts.

5. Drug delivery systems

6. Food processing and storage

7. Air pollution and remediation

8. Construction

9. Health monitoring

10. Vector and pest detection and control

To further assess the impact of nanotechnology on sustainable development, we asked ourselves how well these nanotechnology opportunities matched up with the eight United Nations (UN) Millennium Development Goals, which aim to promote human development and encourage social and economic sustainability. We found that nanotechnology can make a significant contribution to five of the eight goals: eradicating extreme poverty and hunger; ensuring environmental sustainability; reducing child mortality; improving maternal health; and combating AIDS, malaria, and other diseases. A detailed look at how nanotechnology could be beneficial in the three most commonly mentioned areas is illustrative.

Energy Storage, Production, and Conversion

The growing world population needs cheap noncontaminating sources of energy. Nanotechnology has the potential to provide cleaner, more affordable, more efficient, and more reliable ways to harness renewable resources. The rational use of nanotechnology can help developing countries to move toward energy self-sufficiency, while simultaneously reducing dependence on nonrenewable, contaminating energy sources such as fossil fuels. Because there is plenty of sunlight in most developing countries, solar energy is an obvious source to consider. Solar cells convert light into electric energy, but current materials and technology for these cells are expensive and inefficient in making this conversion. Nanostructured materials such as quantum dots and carbon nanotubes are being used for a new generation of more efficient and inexpensive solar cells. Efficient solar-derived energy could be used to power the electrolysis of water to produce hydrogen, a potential source of clean energy. Nanomaterials also have the potential to increase by several orders of magnitude the efficiency of the electrolytic reactions.

One of the limiting factors to the harnessing of hydrogen is the need for adequate storage and transportation systems. Because hydrogen is the smallest element, it can escape from tanks and pipes more easily than can conventional fuels. Very strong materials are needed to keep hydrogen at very low temperature and high pressure. Novel nanomaterials can do the job. Carbon nanotubes have the capacity to store up to 70 percent of hydrogen by weight, an amount 20 times larger than that in currently used compounds. Additionally, carbon nanotubes are 100 times stronger than steel at one-sixth the weight, so theoretically, a 100-pound container made of nanotubes could store at least as much hydrogen as could a 600-pound steel container, and its walls would be 100 times as strong.

Agricultural Productivity Enhancement

Nanotechnology can help develop a range of inexpensive applications to increase soil fertility and crop production and thus to help eliminate malnutrition, a contributor to more than half the deaths of children under five in developing countries. We currently use natural and synthetic zeolites, which have a porous structure, in domestic and commercial water purification, softening, and other applications. Using nanotechnology, it is possible to design zeolite nanoparticles with pores of different sizes. These can be used for more efficient, slow, and thorough release of fertilizers; or they can be used for more efficient livestock feeding and delivery of drugs. Similarly, nanocapsules can release their contents, such as herbicides, slowly and in a controlled manner, increasing the efficacy of the substances delivered.

Water Treatment and Remediation

One-sixth of the world's population lacks access to safe water supplies; one-third of the population of rural areas in Africa, Asia, and Latin America has no clean water; and 2 million children die each year from water-related diseases, such as cholera, typhoid, and schistosomiasis. Nanotechnology can provide inexpensive, portable, and easily cleaned systems that purify, detoxify, and desalinate water more efficiently than do conventional bacterial and viral filters. Nanofilter systems consist of "intelligent" membranes that can be designed to filter out bacteria, viruses, and the great majority of water contaminants. Nanoporous zeolites, attapulgite clays (which can bind large numbers of bacteria and toxins), and nanoporous polymers (which can bind 100,000 times more organic contaminants than can activated carbon) can all be used for water purification.

Nanomagnets, also known as "magnetic nanoparticles" and "magnetic nanospheres," when coated with different compounds that have a selective affinity for diverse contaminating substances, can be used to remove pollutants from water. For example, nanomagnets coated with chitosan, a readily available substance derived from the exoskeleton of crabs and shrimps that is currently used in cosmetics and medications, can be used to remove oil and other organic pollutants from aqueous environments. Brazilian researchers have developed superparamagnetic nanoparticles that, coated with polymers, can be spread over a wide area in dustlike form; these modified nanomagnets would readily bind to the pollutant and could then be recovered with a magnetic pump. Because of the size of the nanoparticles and their high affinity for the contaminating agents, almost 100 percent of the pollutant would be removed. Finally, the magnetic nanoparticles and

Nanotechnology Initiative for Africa and the Caribbean

Africa has rich human and natural resources that are fundamental ingredients to nurture nanotechnology. Africa and the Caribbean like most parts of the world totally lack the physical infrastructures to support nanotechnology. This is the reason why 70,000 well-educated and talented African researchers leave these shores for better research in the developed world. Consequently in about a decade, Africa and the Caribbean will be devoid of any core scientific researchers through this process of brain drain. This problem is more than the HIV/AIDS epidemic or tsunami disaster in Asia. This is the major problem FONAI [Focus Nanotechnology Africa Inc.] is addressing in our proposal for the Nanotechnology Initiative for Africa and the Caribbean.

Mission: Provide educational resources, skilled workforce, and physical infrastructure to enable first-class basic research, exploration of applications, development of new industries, and rapid commercialization of nanotechnology discoveries.

Ejembi Onah,
"Why Africa and the Caribbean Need Nanotechnology,"
Focus Nanotechnology Africa Inc.
(FONAI), 2005.

the polluting agents would be separated, allowing for the reuse of the magnetic nanoparticles and for the recycling of the pollutants. Also, magnetite nanoparticles combined with citric acid, which binds metallic ions with high affinity, can be used to remove heavy metals from soil and water. . . .

Nanotechnology Should Be a Global Effort

Although the ultimate success of harnessing nanotechnology to improve global equity rests with developing countries themselves, there are significant actions that the global community can take in partnership with developing countries to foster the use of nanotechnology for development. These include:

Addressing global challenges. We have proposed an initiative called Addressing Global Challenges Using Nanotechnology, which can catalyze the use of nanotechnology to address critical sustainable development problems. In the spirit of the concept of Grand Challenges, we are issuing a call to arms for investigators to confront one or more bottlenecks in an imagined path to solving a significant development problem (or preferably several) by seeking very specific scientific or technological breakthroughs that would overcome this obstacle. A scientific board, similar to the one created for the Foundation for the U.S. National Institutes of Health/Bill and Melinda Gates Foundation's Grand Challenges in Global Health, with strong representation of developing countries, would need to be established to provide guidance and oversee the program. The top 10 nanotechnology applications identified above can be used as a roadmap to define the grand challenges.

Helping to secure funding. Two sources of funding, private and public, would finance our initiative. In February 2004, Canadian Prime Minister Paul Martin proposed that 5 percent of Canada's R&D investment be used to address developing world challenges. If all industrialized nations adopted this target, part of these funds could be directed toward addressing global challenges using nanotechnology. In addition, developed-country governments should provide incentives for their companies to direct a portion of their R&D toward the development of nanotechnology in less industrialized nations.

Forming effective North-South collaborations. There are already promising examples of North-South partnerships. For instance, the EU [European Union] has allocated 285 million

Euros through its 6th Framework Programme (FP6) for scientific and technological cooperation with third-partner countries, including Argentina, Chile, China, India, and South Africa. A priority research area under FP6 is nanotechnology and nanoscience. Another example is the U.S. funding of nanotechnology research in Vietnam, as well as the U.S.-Vietnam Joint Committee for Science & Technology Cooperation. IndiaNano, a platform created jointly by the Indian-American community in Silicon Valley and Indian experts involved in nanotechnology R&D, aims to establish partnerships between Indian academic, corporate, government, and private institutions in order to support nanotechnology R&D in India and to coordinate the academic, government, and corporate sectors with entrepreneurs, early-stage companies, investors, joint ventures, service providers, startup ventures, and strategic alliances.

Facilitating knowledge repatriation by diasporas. We have recently begun a diaspora study to understand in depth how emigrants can more systematically contribute to innovation and development in their countries of origin. A diaspora is formally defined as a community of individuals from a specific developing country who left home to attend school or find a better job and now work in industrialized nations in academia, research, or industry. This movement of highly educated men and women is often described as a "brain drain" and is usually seen as having devastating effects in the developing world. Rather than deem this migration, which is extremely difficult to reverse, an unmitigated disaster, some developing countries have sought ways to tap these emigrants' scientific, technological, networking, management, and investment capabilities. India actively encourages its "nonresident Indians" diaspora to make such contributions to development back home, and these people have made a valuable contribution to the Indian information technology and communications sector. We foresee a significant role for diasporas in the development of nanotechnology in less industrialized nations.

Emphasizing global governance. We propose the formation of an international network on the assessment of emerging technologies for development. This network should include groups that will explore the potential risks and benefits of nanotechnology, incorporating developed- and developing-world perspectives, and examine the effects of a potential "nanodivide." The aim of the network would be to facilitate a more informed policy debate and advocate for the interests of those in developing countries. Addressing the legitimate concerns associated with nanotechnology can foster public support and allow the technology platform to progress in a socially responsible manner. Among the issues to be discussed are who will control the means of production and who will assess the risks and benefits? What will be the effects of military and corporate control over nanotechnology? How will the incorporation of artificial materials into human systems affect health, security, and privacy? How long will nanomaterials remain in the environment? How readily do nanomaterials bind to environmental contaminants? Will these particles move up through the food chain, and what will be their effect on humans? There are also potential risk management issues specific to developing countries: displacement of traditional markets, the imposition of foreign values, the fear that technological advances will be extraneous to development needs, and the lack of resources to establish, monitor, and enforce safety regulations. Addressing these challenges will require active participation on the part of developing countries. In developing these networks, the InterAcademy Council of the world's science academies could play a role in convening groups of the world's experts who can provide informed guidance on these issues.

Global Inequity Is the Greatest Challenge

The inequity between the industrialized and developing worlds is arguably the greatest ethical challenge facing us today. The gap is even growing by some measures. For example, life expectancies in most industrialized nations are 80 years and rising, whereas in many developed nations, especially in sub-Saharan Africa where HIV/AIDS is rampant, life expectancies are 40 years and falling.

Although science and technology are not a magic bullet and cannot address problems such as geography, poor governance, and unfair trade practices, they have an essential role in confronting these challenges, as explained in the 2005 report of the UN Millennium Project Task Force on Science, Technology and Innovation. Some will argue that the focus on cutting-edge developments in nanotechnology is misplaced when developing countries have yet to acquire more mature technologies and are still struggling to meet basic needs such as food and water availability. This is a short-sighted view. All available strategies, from the simplest to the most complex, should be pursued simultaneously. Some will deal with the near term, others the long-term future. What was cutting-edge yesterday is low-tech today, and today's high-tech breakthrough will be tomorrow's mass-produced commodity.

Each new wave of science and technology innovation has the potential to expand or reduce the inequities between industrialized and developing countries in health, food, water, energy, and other development parameters. Information and communication technology produced a digital divide, but this gap is now closing; genomics and biotechnology spawned the genomics divide, and we will see if it contracts. Will nanotechnology produce the nanodivide? Resources might be directed primarily to nanosunscreens, nanotrousers, and space elevators to benefit the 600 million people in rich countries, but that path is not predetermined. Nanotechnology could soon be applied to address the critical health, food, water, and energy needs of the 5 billion people in the developing world.

> *"Given the current development trajec-*
> *tory of nanotechnology, it appears likely*
> *to exacerbate already existing social in-*
> *equities and create new ones."*

Nanotechnology Will Cause Global Inequity

Georgia Miller and Rye Senjen

In the following viewpoint, Georgia Miller and Rye Senjen argue that nanotechnology will cause significant social disruption and exacerbate global inequities. Miller and Senjen think that it is more likely that nanotechnology will be used to provide products for the rich, not food for the poor. They also think that nanotechnology will eliminate the need for certain commodities, particularly from developing countries, and it will cause millions of laborers to lose their jobs, swelling the ranks of the poor. In the nanofuture envisioned by Miller and Senjen, rich people will use nanotechnology for physical or mental enhancement, distancing themselves further and further from the poor. Miller and Senjen believe that a moratorium on nanotechnology research is needed until measures can be put in place to stave off what they believe are inevitable uses of nanotechnology for the rich at the expense

Georgia Miller and Rye Senjen, "The Disruptive Social Impacts of Nanotechnology," Friends of the Earth Australia, September 2006. Reproduced by permission. http://nano.foe.org.au.

of the poor. Miller is the nanotechnology coordinator and Senjen is the industrial chemicals coordinator for the Friends of the Earth Australia.

As you read, consider the following questions:

1. According to the authors, how much of the U.S. government's nanotechnology research budget in 2006 was allocated to the defense program? How much was allocated to environmental and health impacts?

2. What does the acronym NBIC stand for and what are the authors concerned that it will be used for?

3. How much work in the United States will become unnecessary because of nanotechnology, according to Michael Vassar?

The emerging field of nanotechnology has the potential to bring about changes as big as the European industrial revolution in the late 18th and early 19th century. A hundred and fifty years ago, the mechanization of industry, the introduction of steam power and improved transportation systems brought huge technological, socioeconomic and cultural changes. Today, nanotechnology is forecast to underpin "the next industrial revolution", leading to far-reaching changes in social, economic and ecological relations. Indeed, the Australian National Nanotechnology Strategy Taskforce states that nanotechnology "has the potential to fundamentally alter the way people live". And like the industrial revolution, which took almost 50 years to come to fruition, the impact of nanotechnology is likely to be gradual and almost evolutionary until we find ourselves in the midst of what analysts are predicting will be a "technological tsunami".

Nanotechnology Will Be Associated with Social Upheaval

Proponents and critics alike agree that the real transformative power of nanotechnology lies in its capacity to act as a platform technology, enabling breakthroughs in a wide number of different fields—communications and information technology, cognitive science, biotechnology, agriculture, medicine, manufacturing, energy production, military and environmental remediation to name a few. The ETC Group [Action Group on Erosion, Technology and Concentration, a nonprofit conservation and human rights organization] suggests that: "With applications spanning all industry sectors, technological convergence at the nanoscale is poised to become the strategic platform for global control of manufacturing, food, agriculture and health in the immediate years ahead". The APEC [Asia-Pacific Economic Cooperation] Centre for Technology Foresight observes that major breakthroughs associated with nanoscale convergent technologies will inevitably be associated with large-scale social upheaval. "If nanotechnology is going to revolutionise manufacturing, health care, energy supply, communications and probably defence, then it will transform labour and the workplace, the medical system, the transportation and power infrastructures and the military. None of these latter will be changed without significant social disruption".

The implications of the analysis of such a powerful new technology remain sharply divided. Nano optimists see nanotechnology delivering environmentally benign material abundance for all by providing universal clean water supplies; atomically engineered food and crops resulting in greater agricultural productivity with less labour requirements; nutritionally enhanced interactive 'smart' foods; cheap and powerful energy generation; clean and highly efficient manufacturing; radically improved formulation of drugs, diagnostics and organ replacement; much greater information storage and communication capacities; interactive 'smart' appliances; and increased human performance through convergent technologies.

Nano sceptics suggest that nanotechnology will simply exacerbate problems stemming from existing socioeconomic inequity and the unequal distribution of power by creating greater inequities between rich and poor through a nano-divide; entrenching corporate concentration and enabling its control of even the very building blocks of the natural world; distorting international power relations through its military applications and trade impacts; providing the tools for ubiquitous [seemingly everywhere] surveillance, with significant implications for civil liberty; introducing new and poorly understood risks to the health of humans and the environment; breaking down the barriers between life and non-life, and redefining even what it means to be human.

Nano-Divide Is Inevitable

The consequences of huge global inequities in wealth, power and quality of environment are already starkly evident—poverty, disease and social unrest grip a large proportion of the world's population. Given the current development trajectory of nanotechnology, it appears likely to exacerbate already existing social inequities and create new ones.

A nano-divide appears inevitable. This divide will develop firstly between the nano-poor (most of the world's poorest countries) and the nano-enabled countries. Wealthy countries which are investing in nanotech early—and patenting as quickly as possible—are likely to cement and expand their control of essential manufacturing, industry, agriculture and trade. Poorer countries may find that their products, services and labour are displaced by nano-manufactured goods. A nano-divide is also likely to emerge within each country, as the gap between those who control the new nanotechnologies and those whose products, services or labour are displaced by them, and those who can afford nano enhanced medicines, materials and goods and those that cannot, becomes ever larger. There may also be growing differences between the physical, mental and "performance" abilities of people if plans to "enhance" humans using nanotechnology are realised.

Despite the claims by nanotech proponents that nanotechnology will enable us to eliminate the life-threatening illnesses and hunger of the poor, the huge costs associated with nanotech research demand a focus on profitable applications that will deliver a financial return. Inevitably this will result in medicines, 'smart' foods, new cosmetics and 'smart' appliances for the rich, rather than an effort to reduce the huge inequities in global food distribution and trade that underpin many of the life-threatening illnesses of the poor. Perhaps the most compelling illustration of the fact that nanotechnology's development is being driven by commercial and military interests rather than an altruistic motivation to redress existing social and economic inequity is provided by existing investment and commercialisation trends.

Nanotechnology research is dominated by the military and the first non-military nanoproducts to be released commercially are targeted squarely at wealthy consumers in the Global North. In 2006, the US government, which is the world's biggest funder of nano research, allocated a third of its US$1.3 billion nanotechnology research budget to the US defence program, which was a greater share than that received by the entire National Science Foundation. In stark contrast, research into the environmental and health impacts of nanotechnology received less than 4% of the budget. The first non-military nanoproducts to be released commercially include: anti-ageing cosmetics; odour-eating socks; superior display screens for computers, televisions and mobile phones; premium coatings for luxury cars; and self-cleaning windows and bathrooms. In 2004, the United Kingdom's Royal Society noted that of the engineered nanomaterials in commercial production, the majority were used in the cosmetics industry.

As nanotechnology converges with biotechnology and information technology, patents on atomically modified organisms and materials will increase, as will corporate control of the building blocks of the natural world. As the ETC Group observes: "Despite rosy predictions that nanotech will provide a technical fix for hunger, disease and environmental security in the South, the extraordinary pace of nanotech patenting suggests that developing nations will participate via royalty payments. . . . In a world dominated by proprietary science, it is the patent owners and those who can pay license fees who will determine access and price."

Displacement of Commodities

Very little attention has been paid to studies of the likely disruptive impacts, and massive job losses, associated with the expansion of the near-term nanotechnology industry and its displacement of existing industries. The experience of the European industrial revolution tells us that with rapid technological change come winners, losers and massive social upheaval. Now, as during the previous industrial revolution, it will be the world's poorest people who are least able to adapt quickly in the face of technological change.

In the short-medium term, novel nanomaterials could replace markets for existing commodities, disrupt trade and eliminate jobs in nearly every industry. Industry analysts Lux Research Inc. have warned that nanotechnology will result in large-scale disruption to commodity markets and to all supply and value chains: "Just as the British industrial revolution knocked hand spinners and hand weavers out of business, nanotechnology will disrupt a slew of multi-billion dollar companies and industries".

Technological change and the social disruption it brings has been with us for millennia. What will be different this time is that we are confronting the potentially near simultaneous demise of a number of key commodity markets where raw resources (e.g., cotton, rubber, copper, platinum) may be replaced by nanomaterials, with subsequent structural change to many industry sectors. The displacement of existing commodities by new nanomaterials would have profound impacts for economies everywhere. However, it would have the most devastating impact on people in the Global South whose countries are dependent on trade in raw resources—95 out of 141 developing countries depend on commodities for at least 50% of their export earnings.

Cotton is an example of an important commodity that could be displaced by the introduction of novel nanomaterials. There are currently an estimated 350 million people in the world directly involved in the production of cotton. Countries in the Global South such as Burkina Faso, Benin, Uzbekistan, Mali, Tajikistan, Cote D'Ivoire, Kazakhstan rely on cotton as a major source of revenue. Cotton is also an important export commodity for Australia, worth AUD$1.5 billion in 04/05 making it Australia's 4th largest export commodity. What if 50% of all cotton was replaced by nanofibres? Will government in the Global South have prepared for such an occurrence by supporting the development of new livelihoods for farmers? Or will the price of cotton simply fall to rock bottom and farmers and other cotton workers be left unemployed and suddenly unskilled? What will happen to the Australian cotton industry?

The quest to rebuild life from the atom up, and to replace 'inefficient' primary production with synthetic nanotech alternatives, will also have disastrous economic implications for nations that rely on export or food products. Vandana Shiva [Indian eco-feminist] has argued that synthesising nanotechnology alternatives to food and other natural products will: "accelerate existing trends of patent monopolies over life—making a few corporations 'life-lords'. Most importantly, nanotechnologies and the molecular vision of life will undermine more holistic systems for food and health."

Nano-Enabled Corporate Control of Food, Agriculture and Health

The convergence of technologies at the nano-scale may seem a long way from rural communities in Africa, Asia or Latin America. It is not. More than twenty years ago, we warned that biotechnology would soon affect health and agriculture in developing countries. New technologies in the North also affect markets, imports and exports, labor requirements and production strategies. If the technologies are less than successful, they may be "dumped" in the Third World. If they are commercially successful, they may spill over into developing countries and/or radically transform local economies. With biotechnology, for example, the discovery that farmers' traditional maize varieties in Mexico have been contaminated with genetically modified DNA illustrates the potential health, environmental and trade impacts. The controversy over the shipment of US-grown genetically modified grains as humanitarian food aid to the South provides another example. While the immediate market interest in nano-scale technologies seems strongest in informatics and materials, much work is being done in nano-biotechnology. Just as biotech came to dominate the life sciences over the past two decades, ETC [Erosion, Technology and Concentration] Group believes that nano-scale convergence will become the operative strategy for corporate control of commercial food, agriculture and health in the 21st century.

ETC Group, "The Big Down, Atomtech: Technologies Converging at the Nano-scale," January 2003.

Altering What It Means to Be Human

To an unprecedented degree, the convergence of nanotechnology, biotechnology, robotics and cognitive science offers the potential to dramatically redefine what it is to be human. The quest for biological perfectionism is certainly not new. But the extent of the vision of those who see nanotechnology as our best chance yet to improve human mental, physical and military 'performance' is likely to be shocking for many people in the general community.

The 2002 report *"Converging Technologies for Improving Human Performance: Nanotechnology, Biotechnology, Information Technology and Cognitive Science"* records the proceedings of a high level workshop sponsored by the United States National Science Foundation and the Department of Commerce. The workshop participants envisioned breakthroughs in NBIC [nanotechnology, biotechnology, information technology and cognitive science]-related areas in the next 10 to 20 years that they believed could dramatically enhance the performance of humans. Their vision included the following

- "Fast, broadband interfaces directly between the human brain and machines will transform work in factories, control automobiles, ensure military superiority, and enable new sports, art forms and modes of interaction between people;

- Comfortable, wearable sensors and computers will enhance every person's awareness of his or her health condition, environment, chemical pollutants, potential hazards, and information of interest about local businesses, natural resources, and the like;

- Robots and software agents will be far more useful for human beings, because they will operate on principles compatible with human goals, awareness, and personality;

- The human body will be more durable, healthier, more energetic, easier to repair, and more resistant to many kinds of stress, biological threats, and aging processes;

- A combination of technologies and treatments will compensate for many physical and mental disabilities and will eradicate altogether some handicaps that have plagued the lives of millions of people;

- The ability to control the genetics of humans, animals, and agricultural plants will greatly benefit human welfare; widespread consensus about ethical, legal, and moral issues will be built in the process;

- Factories of tomorrow will be organized around converging technologies and increased human-machine capabilities as 'intelligent environments' that achieve the maximum benefits of both mass production and custom design."

This vision of the future raises profound ethical dilemmas. It is reminiscent of the quest for perfection in the early 20th century by the worldwide eugenics [improvement of the human race through selective breeding] movement and the totalitarian Nazi state of Germany. The ultimate goal of nano-enabled human enhancement is the reconstruction of humans from the atom up. This goal is based on a belief that we can use genetic manipulation and convergent nanoscale technologies to not only increase our mental and physical productivity, but to enable us to integrate with the machines of industry. The claim that a "widespread consensus about ethical, legal, and moral issues will be built in the process" is farcical. Who will decide which of these applications are ethically acceptable or socially desirable? What limits and safeguards will be put on the use of nanobiotechnology, and the engineering of manufactured technological products within biological materials?

The quest to use NBIC technologies to enhance human performance has drawn strong criticism from disabilities and human rights advocates concerned that it will create new inequities and further marginalise existing disadvantaged groups. What efforts will be made to ensure that convergent technology-enabled 'enhancement' of a small number of people in the Global North will not be at the expense of providing basic medicines to the majority of the world's people who still lack access to basic medicines? Will efforts to enhance humans result in further marginalisation of existing marginalised groups, for example disabled people? At what point will the quest to enhance human performance and extend human life produce an elite minority of wealthy, long-living enhanced people, leaving an unenhanced majority underclass?

Displacing People

Fierce debates continue to rage within the nanotechnology industry about whether or not sophisticated molecular manufacturing is possible and achievable. Wishing to avoid a public backlash against "weird science", most in the industry prefer not to speculate about atomically precise manufacturing from decentralised desktop nanofactories. However, given the number of nano-analysts and nano-scientists who predict that molecular manufacturing will be achievable in the next 20–50 years, it is important to give some thought to its potentially devastating implications for human society.

The massive disruptions and disconnects in agriculture, trade, manufacturing, culture and social relations that would accompany such developments are extremely difficult to conceive or comprehend. Using desktop molecular factories would reduce the need for labour in the manufacturing sector to virtually zero. It would also dramatically reduce the need to transport, warehouse or sell goods and would have flow on effects for labour in many associated industries. Michael Vassar [trans humanist] in a recent Center for Responsible Nano-technology (CRN) article, estimated that 60–80% of all work would become unnecessary in the USA within the decade of widespread availability of desktop molecular manufacturing.

What sort of society would we have where 70% of the population did not work? How would this vast group of people feed themselves and meet their basic needs? Would a large part of the population be denied a way of earning a living, becoming dependent on the charity of molecular manufacture? Beyond these basic questions of survival, what would a life dependent on charity without work or the means to purchase non-essential goods mean for people's sense of identity, purpose, self-fulfilment and happiness? Given the scale of potential impacts of molecular manufacturing, it would be reassuring to know that our governments were at least assessing the possibility that it could be developed, rather than dismissing it as impossible.

The current development trajectory of nanotechnology suggests that it will exacerbate existing social inequities and create new ones. There is an urgent need for a moratorium on the commercial research, development, production and release of nanoproducts while we assess the likely extent of nanotechnology's disruptive social impacts, and put measures in place to mitigate these.

Periodical Bibliography

The following articles have been selected to supplement the diverse views presented in this chapter.

Michelle Bryner "Nanotech: Small World Starts to Shrink," *Chemical Week*, August 1, 2007.

Kevin Bullis "Facing the Dangers of Nanotech," *Technology Review*, November 17, 2006. www.technology-review.com.

Ahmed Busnaina "Nanotechnology Enables a Major Manufacturing Paradigm Shift," Smalltimes.com, March 9, 2009. www.smalltimes.com.

Ann Fernholm "Nanoparticles Scrutinized for Health Effects," *San Francisco Chronicle*, May 12, 2008. www.sfgate.com.

Jessica Knoblauch "Whether Nanotechnology Is an Environmental Friend or Foe Remains Unclear," *Plenty Magazine*, July 17, 2008. www.plentymag.com.

Donald C. Maclurcan "Nanotechnology and Developing Countries Part 1: What Possibilities?" *AZojono*, September 30, 2005. www.azonano.com.

Kate Melville "Nanoparticle Laced Wastewater Could Compromise Treatment Plants," *Science A Go Go*, April 30, 2008. www.scienceagogo.com.

Paul Moss "Future Foods: Friend or Foe?" BBC News, February 6, 2007. http://news.bbc.co.uk.

Elizabeth Nord "Top 10 Reasons for Using Nanotech in Food," *Discovery Tech*, February 29, 2009.

ScienceDaily.com "Nanotechnology Boosts Efficiency in Converting Solar Energy into Hydrogen in Fuel Cells," March 22, 2009. www.sciencedaily.com.

What Are the Implications of Molecular Nanotechnology?

Chapter Preface

In 2002, a small group of scientists, worried about the misuse of powerful new technologies, formed an organization called the Lifeboat Foundation. The scientists worried about the misuse of certain emerging technologies, such as nanotechnology, genetic engineering, robotics, and artificial intelligence. They believe that these technologies pose "existential risks." Philosopher and transhumanist Nick Bostrom defines an existential risk as a risk "where an adverse outcome would either annihilate Earth-originating intelligent life or permanently and drastically curtail its potential." Scientists Eric Klien, Jerry Searcy, and others formed the Lifeboat Foundation to educate the public about existential risks and to prevent them from happening.

The Lifeboat Foundation believes that it must be up to scientists to protect humanity from the doomsday scenarios posed by existential risks. Lifeboat does not believe that governments will be able to do it, primarily because they don't think governments worldwide can work together. Additionally, Lifeboat believes that governments tend to act reactively, after events occur, rather than proactively. They believe that existential risks require proactive action because once an existential risk occurs, it will be too late to stop it. According to scientist Ray Kurzweil, an advisory board member of the Lifeboat Foundation, "We cannot rely on trial-and-error approaches to deal with existential risks. . . . We need to vastly increase our investment in developing specific defensive technologies. . . . We are at the critical stage today for biotechnology, and we will reach the stage where we need to directly implement defensive technologies for nanotechnology during the late teen years of this century. . . . A self-replicating pathogen, whether biological or nanotechnology based, could destroy our civilization in a matter of days or weeks."

The existential risk associated with molecular manufacturing is the risk that autonomous self-replicating nanomachines could devour the entire global ecosystem, converting everything—trees, plants, animals, and people—into more nanomachines in a very short time. In his 1986 book on molecular manufacturing, *Engines of Creation*, Eric Drexler warned of the potential for uncontrolled nanomachines, he referred to them as assemblers, "running wild making copies of themselves and ravaging the earth." This scenario was also popularized in the 2002 Michael Crichton novel *Prey*. Lifeboat calls this scenario ecophagy and these nanomachines "ecophages." Lifeboat says that ecophages "would constitute a class of sophisticated artificial life forms more lethal than any plague that has ever existed on this planet. If they are ever built and released, ecophages will need to be controlled by a sophisticated artificial immune system more powerful than any immune system that has appeared in natural biology."

The Lifeboat Foundation proposes "shields" for all existential risks, including ecophages, bioweapons, unfriendly artificial intelligence, and even asteroids. Nanoshield is the name of the program that the Lifeboat Foundation proposes to protect humanity against ecophages. Under Lifeboat's nanoshield proposal, ecophages would be detected and then eradicated. According to Lifeboat, ecophage detection would be difficult, but could be achieved by one of several methods. For instance, detectors could search for the by-products or waste of nanomachines. If ecophages camouflaged their waste, Lifeboat surmises that spectrographic or sonographic detection methods might be used.

Once ecophages were detected, Lifeboat believes that three different lines of defense would be needed to defeat them. The first line of defense would consist of defensive nanorobots that could be deployed to any area that is suspected of having a sign of possible ecophagic activity. These defensive nanorobots would have the ability to disable ecophages by spray painting them to ruin their energy-producing solar cells, physically crushing them, or using electric shock to disable them. The second line of defense would be sent out once the attacking ecophages were identified. This defense would specifically target the particular ecophage and its vulnerabilities. Finally, the Lifeboat Foundation envisions the need for a third and final line of defense, should the first two fail. The third line of defense would need to be so extreme that it would likely cause harm to the world in general. It would only be used if the situation were dire, says the Lifeboat Foundation.

The members of the Lifeboat Foundation believe that humanity needs a nanoshield to protect itself from uncontrolled ecophages. Some scientists, however, do not even believe that nanomachines, or ecophages, are possible and they think the idea of a nanoshield is foolish. The need for protective measures against ecophages is just one of many controversies surrounding the type of nanotechnology called molecular manufacturing. In the following chapter, the authors provide their opinions on other molecular manufacturing issues.

> *"We can see a path to [molecular] assemblers, just at the rocketry pioneers of the 1930s and 1940s could see a path to the Moon."*

Molecular Manufacturing Is Possible

Eric Drexler

In the following viewpoint, Eric Drexler asserts that molecular assemblers will provide the backbone for future manufacturing. The concept of molecular assemblers, or molecular manufacturers, is based on the idea that all manner of products, both organic and inorganic, can be made by assembling atoms together like building blocks. Molecular assemblers are expected to be able to make anything you see in front of you as you're reading this now—a book, a computer, a car, a pencil, a door, a telephone, and even a cup of coffee. Drexler says that chemistry, biology, and engineering show that molecular assemblers are possible. According to Drexler, molecular assemblers are not yet practical, but researchers are making progress and someday they will be a reality. Drexler is an engineer and the author of several books on molecular nanotechnology, including Engines of Creation *and*

Eric Drexler, "Revolutionizing the Future of Technology," EurekaAlert! 2006, www.eurekalert.org. Copyright © 2006 by AAAS. Reproduced by permission. www.eurekalert.org.

Nanosystems. *He was the first scientist to postulate the concept of molecular manufacturing and those who believe in it are often called Drexlerites.*

As you read, consider the following questions:

1. According to Drexler, every manufacturing method is a method for doing what?

2. According to Drexler, engineering shows that precisely made parts can be combined to make what?

3. What is the name of the IBM-developed instrument that enables researchers to observe and move individual atoms and molecules?

The future of technology is in some ways easy to predict. Computers will become faster, materials will become stronger, and medicine will cure more diseases. Nanotechnology, which works on the nanometer scale of molecules and atoms, will be a large part of this future, enabling great improvements in all these technologies. Advanced nanotechnology will work with molecular precision, building a wide range of products that are impossible to make today.

Visions of Nanomachinery and Molecular Manufacturing

When I first introduced a broad audience to the term "nanotechnology" in my 1986 book, *Engines of Creation*, I used it to refer to a vision first described by Richard Feynman in his classic 1959 talk, "There's Plenty of Room at the Bottom." This vision, (expanded upon in technical detail in my 1992 book *Nanosystems: Molecular Machinery, Manufacturing and Computation*), projects the development of productive nanosystems, in other words, nanoscale machinery able to build atomically precise products under digital control. Drawing inspiration from biology, this vision generalizes the nanomachinery of living systems and promises a broad set of productive capabilities with unprecedented power and commensurate opportunities and consequences.

Why focus on productive nanosystems and the large-scale molecular manufacturing processes that they will enable? Because these developments will extend the range of what human beings can manufacture, and through this will change the foundations of physical technology.

Every manufacturing method is a method for arranging atoms. Most methods arrange atoms crudely: even the finest commercial microchips are grossly irregular at the atomic scale, and much of today's nanotechnology faces the same limit. Chemistry and biology, by contrast, make molecules defined by particular arrangements of atoms—always with the same numbers, kinds, and linkages. Chemists use clever methods to do this, but these methods don't scale up well. Biology, however, uses a different, more scalable method: cells contain productive nanosystems (ribosomes) that use digital data (from genes) to guide the assembly of molecular objects (proteins) that they serve as parts of molecular machines. Molecular manufacturing will likewise use stored data to guide construction work done by molecular machines, greatly extending abilities in nanotechnology.

The Molecular Assembler Concept

The basic idea of controlled molecular assembly is simple: where chemists mix molecules in solution, allowing them to wander and bump together at random, molecular assemblers will instead position molecules, bringing them together in a specific position, orientation, and sequence. Letting molecules bump at random leads to unwanted reactions—a problem that grows worse as products get larger. By holding and positioning molecules, assemblers will control how the molecules react, building complex structures with atomically precise control.

Molecular Manufacturing Impossible? Position Unsupportable

The position that molecular manufacturing is impossible is not supportable. Living organisms are not an example of molecular manufacturing, because they are not based on engineering but rather on interlocking complex systems. However, the biochemistry of life could be adapted almost unchanged to a molecular manufacturing system.

A few prominent scientists have nonetheless claimed that molecular manufacturing is impossible, and others have echoed them. However, study of their objections shows that the arguments are weak, based on intuition rather than calculation. Some of the arguments elevate engineering difficulties to the status of fundamental limitations. Others are built on basic misunderstanding of the proposals.

Nanotechnology Now,
"Introduction to Molecular Manufacturing,"
March 29, 2008.

Picture an industrial robot arm standing next to an unfinished workpiece. A conveyor belt supplies the arm with parts, each mounted on a handle. Step after step, the belt advances, the robot grips a fresh handle, plugs the attached part into the workpiece, then puts the empty handle back on the belt. Eventually, the workpiece is finished and another belt moves it away, shifting a new unfinished workpiece into place.

To picture a molecular assembler in a manufacturing system, imagine that all the parts are measured in nanometers, and that the transferred parts are just a few atoms, shifting from handle to workpiece through a chemical reaction at a specific site. An assembler will work as part of a larger system that prepares tools, puts them on the conveyor, and controls the programmable positioning mechanism. Their small moving parts will enable them to operate at high frequencies: because each motion traverses less than a millionth of a meter, each can be completed in less than a millionth of a second. This enables extremely high productivity.

Machines of this sort will be complex systems that are several technology generations away. Indeed, no one is even trying to directly build molecular assemblers today, because nanotechnology is still in its infancy. We can see a path to assemblers, just as the rocketry pioneers of the 1930s and 1940s could see a path to the Moon. But like those pioneers, we aren't ready to attempt the final goal. They knew they must first launch many satellites, just as we must first build many molecular machines. Some of the early machines may resemble the small, simple productive nanosystems that are used today in nature and in biotechnology.

Chemistry, Biology, and Engineering Show the Possibilities

We can catch a glimpse of future technologies because we sometimes can understand things that we can't yet build. Chemistry, biology, engineering and applied physics all provide useful perspectives.

Chemistry shows how structures can form when reactive molecules meet. By using molecular machinery to guide reactive molecules, similar structures can be built at larger scales. The products can be stronger, tougher and more capable than the delicate structures found in living cells.

Biology shows that molecular machines can exist, can be programmed with genetic data, and can build more molecular machines. Biology shows that the products of molecular machine systems can be as low-cost as potatoes. Molecular manufacturing will make a far wider range of products for similarly low costs.

Engineering shows that precisely made parts can be combined to make computers, motors, factories, and a host of useful gadgets. Applied physics, aided by computer modeling, shows that these sorts of devices can be built from atomically precise parts of nanometer scale. These glimpses of future technologies are enough to show some of the potential for molecular manufacturing.

Impacts of Molecular Manufacturing

Molecular manufacturing will bring both great opportunities and great potential for abuse. Advanced systems could be used to build large, complex products cleanly, efficiently, and at low cost. Building with atomic precision, desktop-scale (and larger) manufacturing systems could produce the products like the following, with consequences for many global problems:

- Inexpensive, efficient solar energy systems, a renewable, zero-carbon emission source

- Desktop computers with a billion processors

- Medical devices able to destroy viruses and cancer cells without damaging healthy cells

- Materials 100 times stronger than steel

- Superior military systems

- More molecular manufacturing systems

Faster, cheaper, cleaner production of superior products will also be disruptive. Costs, resource requirements and economic organization will be transformed. Advanced lethal and non-lethal weapons, deployed quickly and cheaply, could make the world a more dangerous place. The list of potential consequences is long, and as with all powerful technologies, the results will depend on the intent of the users.

Progress Toward Future Nanosystems

In laboratories around the world, researchers are developing useful products and providing instruments, techniques and nanoscale components that will enable the development of future productive nanosystems.

We have seen steady advances in understanding and controlling atoms, molecules and atomically precise structures. Some instruments now enable researchers to observe and move individual atoms and molecules. The most widely known of these is the scanning tunneling microscope (STM), first developed by researchers at IBM Zurich's labs.

We have also seen progress in building novel structures along the lines proposed in my 1981 paper in the *Proceedings of the National Academy of Sciences*. This is the field of protein engineering which, together with DNA engineering, has demonstrated design and synthesis or atomically precise molecular objects like those that function as components of the molecular machinery, processing and electronics in biology.

Another area of rapid progress is computational modeling. Advances in hardware and software enable design and simulation-based testing of molecular devices, giving results with greater accuracy for structures on larger scales. This progress is crucial to the development of molecular systems engineering.

In considering these goals and accomplishments, it is important to distinguish long-term promise from present-day capabilities. Developing advanced productive nanosystems will require a multi-stage process in which today's laboratory capabilities are used to build molecular tools with broader capabilities. These tools, in turn, will be used in the next stage of development. Nanotechnology using productive nanosystems and their products will build on and extend the nanotechnologies of today, enabling a progressively broader range of applications.

The research that will support these developments is underway in laboratories in every industrial country. Unlike past revolutions in technology, the U.S., Europe and Asia are all making similar progress.

"Nanosystems *is, in the kindest view, a thought experiment carried far too far.*"

Molecular Manufacturing Is Impossible

William Illsey Atkinson

In the following viewpoint, William Illsey Atkinson argues that Eric Drexler's concept of molecular assemblers—set out in his 556-page book Nanosystems—*is not scientifically workable. Atkinson says Drexler's vision of tiny nanobots assembling any sort of thing possible—a car, chewing gum, cancer drugs, a bridge—is grandiose. Atkinson maintains that Drexler's entire concept of molecular manufacturing is based on the incorrect assumption that the laws of physics that govern the "macrocosm" will govern the "nanocosm." Atkinson believes Drexler is a charismatic leader, but he doesn't think much of his scientific expertise and he thinks his vision of molecular assemblers is a sham. Atkinson is a scientific writer, author of several books, and president of Draaken Communications, which interprets technological issues for universities, institutes, and private firms.*

As you read, consider the following questions:

1. According to Atkinson, what does Drexler call his "fifth state of existence?"

2. According to Atkinson, making a machine is just the beginning of a workable technology. What are some of the things you must do after you make the machine?

3. According to Atkinson, what did Albert Einstein say about common sense?

"K. Eric Drexler published the first scientific paper on molecular nanotechnology in 1981. In addition, he taught the first course on the subject [at Stanford University] and chaired the first two conferences [on nanotech]. He is currently President of the Foresight Institute [now chairman of the board] and a Research Fellow of the Institute for Molecular Manufacturing. He wrote *Nanosystems* while a Visiting Scholar at the Stanford University Department of Computer Science and continues to lecture at universities and corporations in the U.S., Europe, and Japan. He received his doctoral degree in molecular nanotechnology from MIT." [—Jacket biography from *Nanosystems: Molecular Machinery, Manufacturing, and Computation* (New York: John Wiley & Sons, Inc., 1992)]

There you have him: K. Eric Drexler. The guy who took up the gauntlet Dick Feynman threw down to the scientific-engineering establishment in 1959. The linguistic genius who coined the word *nanotechnology* as a brilliant parallel of *microtechnology*: the same concept, but a thousand times as small. The lone visionary who risked certain derision from the established authorities and dared to dream. And not only to dream, but to dream the way a reputable engineer does it: not merely in words but in numbers. A quantifying dreamer like Edison or Newton or Feynman himself. A pioneer, a Brigham

Young, who surrounded himself with a coterie [group] of the like-minded and welded them into a movement that shook the world.

Dr. Ralph Merkle, for example. Ten years ago Dr. Merkle was a high-profile cryptographer, a member of the research staff in the Computational Nanotechnology Project at PARC—Xerox Corporation's Palo Alto Research Center. Then Eric Drexler moved west to study there. Now Dr. Merkle is vice president of technology assessment at the Foresight Institute, a nonprofit organization formed in 1986 by Drexler and Christine Peterson (a.k.a. Mrs. K. Eric Drexler). At the 2002 Nanotech Planet World Conference in San José, Ralph Merkle gave the second day's keynote address. Two days before that, Merkle's colleague Neil Jacobstein, chairman of the Molecular Manufacturing Institute and an affiliate of the Foresight Institute, gave conference delegates a briefing on what nanotechonology is, where it came from, and where it's going.

Impossible to Ignore

In Jacobstein's vision, which is orthodox Drexlerianism, K. Eric is front and center—and necessarily so. Drexler is to the nanoboosters as Christ is to the Christians.... Most people would agree with this assessment, even when Drexler's views and opinions fill them with skepticism, vague unease, or disagreement amounting to loathing. Love him or hate him, Drexler is impossible to ignore.

Scientific American, doyen of U.S. popular science periodicals and a magazine so revered that *Esquire* once satirized its motto as "Founded A.D. 11," gave Drexler a two-page inside spread in its September 2001 special issue. That's more than *SciAm* gives to some Nobel laureates. In this article Drexler synopsizes arguments set out at length in his more scholarly books, especially the 556-page tome *Nanosystems*. In *SciAm* Drexler takes up where Feynman left off. A few excerpts catch the tenor of his *SciAm* message:

"It would be a natural goal to be able to put every atom in a selected place ... with no extra molecules on the loose to jam the works. Such a system would not be a liquid or gas, as no molecules would move randomly, nor would it be a solid, in which molecules are fixed in place." Drexler calls this new, fifth state of existence "machine-phase matter." It will, he says, be characterized by nanoscale machines creating things from the bottom up, atom by atom: new drugs, synthetic materials with vast structural efficiencies, and even copies of themselves—robots building robots building etc.

All this would lead to what you'd have to call an RIE, a Revolution in Everything. Transportation would improve; colonizing near-space and other planetary surfaces would become cost-efficient. Most striking of all, "medical nanorobots ... could destroy viruses and cancer cells, repair damaged structures, remove accumulated wastes from the brain and bring the body back to a state of youthful health."

Even an RIE is just the beginning. As Drexler sees it, machine-phase nanotech would give us "the eventual ability to repair and revive those few pioneers now in suspended animation (currently regarded as legally deceased), even those who have been preserved using the crude cryogenic storage technology available since the 1960s." [I love the term coined by sci-fi author Larry Niven for these latter-day undead: "corpsicles."]

Concluding his *SciAm* piece, Drexler admits that the Shangri-la he depicts, while on its way, won't happen overnight. He sees "the technology base underpinning such capabilities as perhaps one to three decades off."

Note that the RIE that Drexler prophesies will be neither chemical nor biological, but mechanical. Everything will be accomplished by little machines, much like those we see today whipping about on robotic assembly lines, but smaller—way, way smaller. The Drexlerian "nanobot," he confidently asserts, will be one million to ten million times smaller in diameter than current mechanisms: in volume, one trillion to one quadrillion times more tiny. One quadrillion is the number of quarts of water in Lake Superior.

Nanosystems, the book behind this astounding summary, is not what you'd call a light summer read. Given its mind-numbing opacity, it's hard to see why this book is so effective at raising the hackles of many mainstream scientists. Sample text: "The variations in the potential V(x) associated with sliding a component over a surface can in the standard molecular mechanics approximations be decomposed into a sum of the pairwise nonbonded potentials between the atoms in the object and those in the surface together with terms representing variations in the internal strain energy of the object and the surface." That's not exactly "Arise ye prisoners of starvation" or "We hold these truths to be self-evident," but it's compelling to a certain subset of mechanical engineers. *Nanosystems* has become a classic, at least in Mark Twain's definition: "A book that people praise and don't read." Even people who swear by it, or at it, have rarely gone through this brick of a book cover to cover.

So detailed is Drexler's exegesis [analysis] that its sheer mass can start to sway you: Your eyes glaze over at the scope of it all. Surely all this amazing technical erudition must lead somewhere? In a kind of *argumentum ad hominum, technocratium* [attacking the source of an argument instead of argument itself], you ask yourself: How could anyone so learned be wrong? "Almost thou persuadest me to be a Drexlerian."

Too Many Doubts

And then the niggling doubts enter your mind. To begin with, making a machine is just the beginning of a workable technology: You must also maintain it. You must control all the separate parts of your machine, mastering matter at scales ten

Drexler's Bedtime Story

A few weeks ago I gave a talk on nanotechnology and energy titled "Be a Scientist, Save the World" to about 700 middle and high school students in the Spring Branch ISD, a large public school system here in the Houston area. Leading up to my visit, the students were asked to write an essay on "Why I Am a Nanogeek." Hundreds responded, and I had the privilege of reading the top 30 essays, picking my favorite five. Of the essays I read, nearly half assumed that self-replicating nanobots were possible, and most were deeply worried about what would happen in their future as these nanobots spread around the world. I did what I could to allay their fears, but there is no question that many of these youngsters have been told a bedtime story that is deeply troubling.

You and people around you have scared our children. I don't expect you to stop, but I hope others in the chemical community will join with me in turning on the light, and showing our children that, while our future in the real world will be challenging and there are real risks, there will be no such monster as the self-replicating mechanical nanobot of your dreams.

Sincerely,

RICK SMALLEY

"Nanotechnology: Drexler and Smalley Square Off,"
Chemical & Engineering News, *December 1, 2003.*

to a thousand times smaller than the scale of your overall invention. To make a building, you must make, lay, and maintain its bricks.

Take a standard industrial robot used on an assembly line, say, 2 x 2 x 1 meters in size. To fabricate this, and then to service it, you will need to control factors all the way from the submicron range (e.g., metallurgical microstructure) up to the half-meter size of the major parts, and everything in between. What happens when a nanobot breaks down? Who squirts oil or its nano-equivalent into lube nipples, or remachines bearings, or sharpens tools? Don't tell me it won't or it can't fail: It must, unless Drexlerianism admits itself to be outright theology.

Consider a soberly presented Drexlerian "invention" such as the Stiff-Arm Nanomanipulator. Here in a package only 100 nm high we see a robotic arm with telescopic and rotary joints, core plates, drive gears, snap-on attachments that transport and handle tools, and complex intersegmental bearings. Some of these parts are fifteen angstroms across. Essentially it's a robot from a General Motors assembly line shrunk one hundred million diameters. Beyond that, no concessions are made to the *otherness* of the nanocosm, about which we are only starting to learn—the nano-realm's vast difference from our macroworld.

In essence, Drexler does an amazingly thorough job of assuming that the nanocosm will prove to be just like the macrocosm, only smaller. He then expends an equally amazing amount of energy, insight, and erudition expanding on this initial, wrong assumption. On p. 327 of his book, for example, he writes: "An approximation for the pressure gradient along a tube containing a fluid in turbulent flow is the Darcy-Weisbach formula . . . where v is the mean velocity of the fluid, and f is a friction factor that depends on the Reynolds number R of the flow and the roughness of the wall. The parameter f can be evaluated by methods described in Tapley and Poston (1990); a high value (for a rough pipe at low R) is 0.1, a low value (for a smooth pipe at R>10') is 0.008."

The exactness of this analysis is impressive. There's only one problem: We don't yet know if it's right. Odds are good, in fact, that it's a half-bubble off level. Corrections such as the

Reynolds number are entirely empirical. They were derived, refined, and verified by close observation of how the macro-world behaves, Drexler almost never presents truly theoretical explanations for such correction factors. They work, is all—at least at the macroscale. But at the nanoscale, a totally different world presents itself for our understanding. And the nano-cosm is not by any means a world we understand. When a pipe is <1 nm in internal diameter, for example—as a single-walled carbon nanotube is—we have no way of knowing if anything other than electrons will flow through it in classical patterns. It's more likely that the well-known stickiness of the tube's carbon atoms will instantly immobilize any material within. We cannot even use macroscale, commonsense terms such as *fluid* at nanometer dimensions. Many organic mol-ecules that constitute fluids in the macroscale would be too big to fit inside a buckytube. If they did squeeze in, they'd quickly jam. Even molecules that would theoretically fit (diatomic hydrogen, for instance, which measures only a quar-ter of a nanometer edge to edge) would not necessarily behave in a typically fluidic way inside a nanotube—at least not as a top-notch empirical scientist like Reynolds would have under-stood the term fluidic. In the nanocosm, a bundle of H2 mol-ecules would act like a collection of solid, incompressible nodes; they would be no more fluidic than boulders rolling through a trash can.

Even in the macroscale, gases and fluids vastly alter their behavior when key parameters change. To the aircraft de-signer, the thinner air found in the stratosphere no longer be-haves as a classical gas, nor does it exhibit classical fluid-like properties. Aeronautical engineers have learned through hard experience that they must treat ultrahigh-altitude air not as a gas but as a "flux"—that is, a barrage of discrete particles. This numerically measurable change results from change in a single thing: air density.

Theorizing Is Useless

The moral is clear. You cannot assume that the undiscovered realm of the nanocosm will be just like your kitchen counter. You have to go and find out how things in the nanocosm behave. Otherwise your theorizing is so much fluff.

Drexler, unheeding, proclaims the nanocosm to be SOS, Same Only Smaller. All we have to do is take the machinery we see around us, and shrink it. Itty-bitty bulldozers. Molecule-sized manipulators. Conveyor belts that lug a couple of atoms at a time. Drexler even proposes a wholesale return to the Babbage Difference Engine, performing computations at the nanoscale with cams and push rods. Nano-abacus, anyone? There are flywheels for energy buffering, with radii of 195 nm and a rim velocity of 1,000 m/s, which I calculate would give the nano-flywheel a spin rate of fifty million RPM!

No two ways about it: There's no timidity in the man. Here's Martin Amis on Norman Mailer: "He is never afraid to risk looking like a fool. Though perhaps someone should explain to him that there is a role for fear."

No. Something about the whole Drexlerian school sets off alarm bells all over my brain. Drexler could be exactly what his acolytes think: one of those crowning visionaries that comes along every century or so, someone who sees so far ahead that when he reports back what he's seen, we groundlings think he's bonkers. The da Vinci of our time. That's what he has a chance of being—maybe. Still, I live by Hemingway's dictum: "The most essential gift for a good writer is a built-in shock-proof shit-detector." And in this case, to use an analogy spoken by the very moderator who introduced Dr. Merkle, the needle on my B.S. meter has swung over so far that it's resting on the pin.

Here's my own take on Drexlerian nanotech. I don't think Drexler has established an engineering school at all. Reputable schools undertake original research, then present their findings in peer-reviewed journals and colloquia. They limit their predictions to short extrapolations of current work. These extrapolations must be technically rigorous and mathematically defensible. Sound, solid schools do *not* indulge in wild fantasies and they do *not* put vast effort into persuading the laity via PR. Instead, they try to sway a knowledgeable élite with watertight argument. "The world," Sir Thomas More said at his trial, "must construe according to its wits; this court"—the court of science—"must construe according to the [natural] law."

A casual reading of *Nanosystems* is all it takes to trigger the alarms. This is a utopian vision, and as G.K. Chesterton said of utopias, they first assume that no one will want more than his fair share, and then are ingenious in explaining how that share will be delivered to them via balloon. Utopias, in other words, are skillfully built on iffy foundations. Even when their upper structures are well carpentered, the footings that support them won't pass close inspection. However good a utopia may seem, it's built to impress and not to last.

Drexler tries to have it both ways. He wants the unfettered freedom of the blackboard jockey, the absolute liberty of the theoretician, whose mind roams time and space at will. On top of that, he wants the rigor of the experimentalist who presents to us the nature he or she observes and dares us to challenge its reality. Unfortunately, Drexler vies for these distinctions without meeting the standards and qualifications of either. *Nanosystems,* and the doctoral studies on which it's based, constitute a kind of spadework. With them, Drexler shows the engineering world the stick-to-itiveness and the "fine ratiocinative meditativeness" that are the engineer's equivalent of piety. He demonstrates his willingness to boldly go where no man has gone before—including skating on ice so thin it's imaginary. He's an experimentalist who hasn't done and won't do experiments, a theoretician brilliantly connecting data that have never been derived. Drexler says he's invented an entire new field, or rather a field full of fields. He calls it "theoretical applied science." Yet Drexler isn't summarizing what he, or anyone else, has ever seen. He's what-iffing, on grounds as nebulous as common sense—what *should* exist at the nanoscale, once we look. There's a word for what Walt Disney called the "plausible impossible." It's *specious*.

I prefer the more learned and modest approach of one A. Einstein, a more substantial scientist than K. Eric Drexler. Einstein defined common sense as the set of prejudices that we accrete before age eighteen. He cautioned against using this as a guide in the extreme worlds we enter when, through laboratory experiment or else the thought experiments of imagination, we accelerate up toward lightspeed or shrink down to the nanocosm. Common sense, it turns out, is neither common nor sensible outside the macroworld in which it was learned—and in which, and *only* in which, it applies. Yet here's Drexler, Our Founder, blithely traipsing through a world of quantum weirdness as if it's a backyard barbecue in Redwood City. Mechanosynthesis of diamondoid! Nanoscale symmetrical-sleeve bearings! Nuts and screws and rods in sleeves! Gears and rollers, belts and cams! Dampers, detents, clutches, and ratchets! Drives, fluids, seals, pumps, and cooling systems! Electrostatic motors—and here I have to say, as the musical comedienne Anna Russell says about the libretti of Richard Wagner: "I'm not making this up, you know."

Too Many Technical Gaps

The unease you feel when you consider the technical gaps in Drexler's intellectual fabric increases a hundredfold when you examine the means that he and his followers have chosen to propagate their beliefs. Consider the rhetorical technique called poisoning the well. In a single paragraph called "Criticism of Criticism" (p. xviii of the introduction to *Nanosystems*), Drexler airily dismisses all possible objections to his ideological constructs out of hand. He states that his approach of molecular manufacturing will work if he's given inflexible molecules, nonreactive atoms, stable fragments, and a total absence of any trace contaminants. But in so doing, Drexler immediately paints himself into a corner. His own constraint-set obviates his predicted inventions, such as the nanoassembler or the blood-cruising medical nanobot that repairs cells as they age. (We'd love to help, sir, but first your liver must be made from diamond.) His nanobots will sense their surroundings but not see them; they will not be subject to dislocation by thermal motion; their work will produce no excess heat, etc.

Nanosystems is, in the kindest view, a thought experiment carried far too far. At first it seems the product of a bright, unbridled mind, which like Stephen Leacock's famous general mounts a horse and gallops madly off in all directions. But is Drexler really that sophomoric or self-deluded? On deeper consideration I'd say no. His real goal, I think, was to establish himself as *the* expert in a new high-profile area, without the bother of original experiment or rigorous, cautious, defensible interpretation. And this he has most certainly done. He's certainly enlisted a mass of followers. To a certain stripe of pop-sci, New Age nanobooster, the kind that entertainingly infests Web sites like *planet.hawaii.com*, Drexler stands serene and solitary as Our Founder. Even reputable scientists must acknowledge this achievement, though they cannot quite fathom how or why it occurred.

> *"We are on the cusp of a new era that has the potential to be an era of abundance. In the coming decades, molecular manufacturing will be a reality."*

Molecular Nanotechnology Can Bring Abundance to All Mankind

Steven G. Burgess

In the following viewpoint, Steven G. Burgess contends that molecular manufacturing has the potential to reduce the threat of war, increase the quality of life, and bring abundance to humans around the world. According to Burgess, wars typically break out when people fight over scarce resources. If personal nanofactories become a reality, and Burgess believes they will, then everyone will be able to have abundant food, water, and other resources, thus ending one of the primary reasons for war. Burgess thinks politicians and corporations who profit under the current system of scarcity will be reluctant to let go of their current edge. He be-

Steven G. Burgess, "The (Needed) New Economics of Abundance," Nanotechnology Now, March 29, 2008. www.nanotech-now.com. Copyright © 1999–2008 7thWave, Inc. All rights reserved. Reproduced by permission.

lieves, however, the world must strive toward this vision of molecular manufacturing abundance. Burgess is an expert in computer forensics and a senior fellow at the Foresight Nanotech Institute.

As you read, consider the following questions:

1. According to Burgess, economics textbooks, such as *Principles of Economics*, don't mention what word?

2. According to World Bank estimates, how many humans live below a level necessary to meet basic needs?

3. According to Burgess, the chairman of what major company is calling for the government to incentivize his industry to produce an environmentally friendly product?

For centuries, we have built cultures and economies around scarcity. Economics is the "study of how human beings allocate scarce resources" in the most efficient way and conventional wisdom agrees that regulated capitalism results in the most efficient allocation of those scarce resources.

An Era of Abundance

But what happens if resources are not scarce? What economic system would we use to allocate plentiful resources? Is there even a point to talking about the "economics of abundance" in a culture where economic equations are entirely oriented around scarcity? As Chris Anderson, editor of *Wired* magazine says, "My college textbook, Gregory Mankiw's otherwise excellent *Principles of Economics*, doesn't mention the word abundance. And for good reason: If you let the scarcity term in most economic equations go to nothing, you get all sorts of divide-by-zero problems. They basically blow up."

We are on the cusp of a new era that has the potential to be an era of abundance. In the coming decades, molecular manufacturing will be a reality. *The Nanotechnology Glossary*

American Living Standards for the World

Most men have been slaves of necessity, while the few who were not lived by exploiting others who were. Although mechanization has eased that burden in the advanced countries, it is still the case for the majority of the human race. Limited resources (mainly fossil fuels), as well as negative consequences of industrialization such as global warming, have made some people question whether American living standards can ever be extended to most of the human race. . . .

Hardly anyone seems to realize it, but we're on the threshold of an era of unbelievable abundance. Within a generation—sooner if we want it enough—we will be able to make a self-replicating machine.

Gregory Cochran, "The Sorcerer's Apprentice," Edge: World Question Center, January 2007. http://edge.org.

defines molecular manufacturing as "the automated building of products from the bottom up, molecule by molecule, with atomic precision. This will make products that are extremely lightweight, flexible, durable, and potentially very 'smart.'" And cheap. Just as Apple enabled personal publishing by marrying the Postscript language with the Macintosh interface and an inexpensive LaserWriter printer, so will the coupling of molecular manufacturing with appropriate programming tools bring about a revolution we might call "personal manufacturing." Such personal nanofactories (PNs) already have been envisioned and are likely to be similar in look and ease of use to a printer or microwave oven. Indeed, an artist's conception can be seen online.

Personal Nanofactories Bring Down Costs

The advent of PNs should bring the cost of most nonfood necessities to near zero. Much of the raw material for most objects we commonly use can be found in air and dirt, with a few fortified materials thrown in. If we build things from the molecules up (and conversely, break things down into their component molecules for reuse), materials cost will nearly disappear. Information would then become the most expensive resource.

Meanwhile, computing power—information management—continues to expand exponentially even as its cost drops precipitously. Furthermore, as true artificial intelligence (AI) approaches, computers will become self-programming, and information cost may drop even more dramatically. It's already happening. Today, most of our products contain greater and greater information content (technology) at lesser and lesser cost. It appears that even food eventually could be manufactured on the kitchen countertop personal nanofactory at practically no materials cost.

However, if history is a guide, the "haves" will always want to have more and the "have-nots" will end up getting relatively less. That is the way many people keep score—as the bumper sticker wisdom goes, "He who dies with the most toys wins." It's not just a silly ditty. It is a frank statement of the mindset of many individuals. And it is the "haves" that possess easy access to the levers of power and legislation. In a system based on scarcity, those holding the levers of production will not easily give them up. In domestic and international markets based on scarcity, the function and responsibility of directors and officers is to maximize shareholder value—at nearly any cost that does not fall afoul of laws, or at least not so far afoul that the penalties exceed the financial gain resulting from illegal actions.

Molecular Manufacturing Can End War and Poverty

So, what kind of culture do we want? In a system of plenty, will we continue to keep score by maintaining the preponderance of benefits inside corporate walls and coffers? Will we continue to stifle the spread of benefits through secrecy and protectionism? Unless something changes, history suggests that laws, regulations, and protections will continue to be designed for the exact purpose of directing all profits and virtually all of the benefits to shareholders.

Is it possible to change this historical trend? Is it desirable? What would an economy based on abundance look like? What would we call it? Could we convince the lawmakers, the regulators, and those who currently benefit most from a system based on scarcity to relinquish what has worked so well for them?

I maintain that it is desirable and that we must drive toward an outcome whereby the benefits of molecular manufacturing accrue to the greatest number of people. War, poverty, and business drive my reasoning.

To date, all our technological and economic progress has produced a world at war and in poverty. War is largely fought over scarce resources. Widespread wealth (through universal distribution of PNs) would remove the apparent fuel for most wars.

The World Bank estimates that 2.7 billion humans live below a level necessary to meet basic needs. The organization says that this kind of poverty includes hunger, lack of shelter, no access to medicines, and losing a child to illness brought about by unclean water. Few would argue that human misery is desirable. PNs could be programmed to provide basic building supplies, medicine, foodstuffs, and clean water.

Convincing Corporations to Share

As regards business, I believe we can convince a wide range of enterprises, from local to transnational, that maximizing the benefits for billions of people (read: "customers") simultaneously maximizes value for shareholders . . . in the long run.

However, nearly all businesses act primarily in the interest of the short term. Corporate directors cannot allow a departure from known short-term profit centers in the market without assistance from legislation and regulators to flatten the playing field for all. Even Bill Ford, chairman of the Ford Motor Company, is calling for government to incentivize his industry to produce environmentally friendly technology—ostensibly, so his firm can afford to produce such vehicles while staying competitive with other auto manufacturers.

We must incentivize, strongly encourage, or require the broad sharing of the benefits of early-onset molecular manufacturing advances and breakthroughs so that the long-term benefits can be realized. This discussion needs to happen now, before entrenched interests develop protections and harden regulations adapted for maximum short-term profits while stifling innovation. Market forces can be too slow. What's needed is a means to produce broad and inexpensive licensing so that early breakthroughs in molecular manufacturing can quickly benefit a broad swath of humanity.

Over hundreds of years, we have developed the skills of how to allocate things in short supply. For widespread abundance, we have no experience, no projections, and no economic calculations. Abundance, paradoxically, could be highly disruptive. It is time to design a new economics of abundance, so that abundance can be enjoyed in a society that is prepared for it.

> "Imagine a scenario in which a single individual in possession of unrestricted technology and resources could conquer the entire world. This will be our world in the era of molecular manufacturing."

Molecular Nanotechnology Will Lead to the End of the World

Britt Gillette

In the following viewpoint, Britt Gillette discusses molecular manufacturing's role in the end of the world. According to Gillette, molecular manufacturing and its potential as a weapon of mass destruction will lead to a massive and unstable molecular manufacturing arms race between several countries. Gillette believes that one country will emerge the winner and this country will control the entire world. According to Gillette, the Bible predicts such events. The Bible says that in the end, one country will control the world and the leader of this country will be the

Britt Gillette, "Why Global Government Is Inevitable," Brittgillette.com, October 30, 2007. Reproduced by permission.

Antichrist. Soon after the Antichrist takes power, the world will end and Jesus Christ will reappear. Gillette is a blogger and author of several books about Bible prophesies and emerging technologies.

As you read, consider the following questions:

1. According to Gillette, international stability has been built on the concept of Mutually Assured Destruction since when? What happened in that year?

2. According to Gillette and the Center for Responsible Nanotechnology, what are the differences between nuclear weapons and nanocapability that makes a nuclear arms race stable and a molecular manufacturing arms race unstable?

3. According to Gillette, a global government must maintain constant vigilance toward the threat of an emerging power. This will require what, according to Gillette?

According to the Bible, in the last days, a unified global government will rule the world. The head of this global government, the Antichrist, is one of the more infamous figures in human history, and not a single individual on the face of the earth will lie outside of his jurisdiction:

> "And he was given authority to rule over every tribe and people and language and nation."
>
> *Revelation 13:7*

This global government will emerge in our generation because current technological trends will soon make it inevitable. The catalyst for this consolidation of global political power will be the development of molecular manufacturing (MM), a revolutionary technology of unprecedented capability and strength. It's a technology that could arrive as soon as tomorrow and almost certainly will arrive within the next decade.

Molecular Manufacturing and Geopolitical Instability

International relations since World War II have largely been shaped by the existence of nuclear weapons. Likewise, the era to come will largely be shaped by the existence of molecular manufacturing. The development of MM will have a much more significant impact than the development of atomic weapons, and the stakes will be much higher. This is because world domination could easily be achieved with the creation of molecular manufacturing.

MM is the ability to manufacture products from the bottom up, one molecule at a time, with atomic precision. The development of MM will lead to the creation of the personal nanofactory, a desktop appliance capable of creating everyday products from basic feedstock (molecules). The consequences of such a technology are so profound, they are probably beyond the ability of a single individual to comprehend.

Since a nanofactory is capable of self-replication, the first could manufacture a duplicate copy of itself. Those two then become four, become eight, and so on. As a result, this compounding capital base could create a massive and decisive military force within days. As Dr. K. Eric Drexler described in his book, *Engines of Creation*, "a state that makes the assembler breakthrough could rapidly create a decisive military force—if not literally overnight, then at least with unprecedented speed."

Molecular Manufacturing and Mutually Assured Destruction

Since the Soviet Union emerged as the world's second nuclear power in 1949, international stability has been built on the concept of Mutually Assured Destruction (MAD). The prospect of MAD has successfully prevented the eruption of World War III by making a potential military conflict between nuclear powers equally undesirable to each party involved.

This has led many to believe that victory in such a conflict is unattainable. With current technology, this assumption is probably correct. However, once molecular manufacturing emerges, this will no longer be true. A MM-enabled power could easily circumvent MAD.

A nation in possession of nanofactories is capable of rapidly manufacturing and deploying billions of microscopic/macroscopic machines at relatively little cost. These machines could comb the oceans for enemy submarines and quickly disable the nuclear arsenals they carry. Similar acts of sabotage could be carried out simultaneously against land-based nuclear facilities and conventional military forces in a matter of hours, if not minutes. Rendering its enemies utterly defenseless, the MM-enabled nation could conquer at will without fear of nuclear retaliation.

Molecular Manufacturing Arms Race

The development of molecular manufacturing opens the door for its initial user to completely dominate world affairs. A nation equipped with contemporary technology attempting to defend itself against a MM-enabled nation is akin to a small band of cavemen armed with rocks and spears attempting to overpower a modern day army. Given the stakes involved, it's reasonable to believe multiple nations are currently in pursuit of a molecular manufacturing capability—just as Germany, Japan, and the United States covertly and simultaneously pursued the creation of an atomic bomb.

If Germany had been the first to succeed in the development of atomic weaponry, it's almost certain that Hitler would've used this advantage to drive the Allied Forces from the European Continent, perhaps totally defeating the United States in the process. In contrast, the United States, as the world's first nuclear power, could've used its position to prevent rival nations from acquiring the same capability. In fact, the United States could've used its position to create an impregnable world empire.

In similar fashion, the leading MM-enabled nation can create its own empire if it uses its initial advantage to prevent competing nation states from developing a molecular manufacturing capability of their own. However, in all probability, this is not just one of several options, but the only option. Unlike the nuclear era, the prospect of MM proliferation is simply intolerable.

This is because of the inherent instability of an arms race between competing MM-enabled nation states. This nightmarish prospect is identified by the Center for Responsible Nanotechnology [CRN] as one of the foremost dangers posed by molecular manufacturing:

> "The nuclear arms race was stable for several reasons. In virtually every way, the nano-arms race will be the opposite. Nuclear weapons are hard to design, hard to build, require easily monitored testing, do indiscriminate and lasting damage, do not rapidly become obsolete, have almost no peaceful use, and are universally abhorred. Nanocapability will be easy to build (given a nanofactory), will allow easily concealable testing, will be relatively easy to control and deactivate, would become obsolete very rapidly, almost every design is dual-use, and peaceful and non-lethal (police) use will be common. Nukes are easier to stockpile than to use; nanoweapons are the opposite."

Options for the Arms Race Winner

CRN also agrees that a molecular manufacturing monopoly will be an attractive policy option for the nation that first develops molecular manufacturing:

> "Each nation will see only a few possibilities: 1) an arms race that will probably be unwinnable since it will develop into a disastrous war; 2) developing ahead of everyone else

Protecting Ourselves from Ourselves

Molecular manufacturing will give its wielders extreme power—certainly enough power to overcome all significant non-human limits (at least within the context of the planet; in space, there will be other limits such as scarcity of materials and speed of light). Even if the problem of cheaters could be overcome, we do not have many internal limits these days; the current trend in capitalism is to deny the desirability of all limits except those that arise from competition. What's left?

Somehow, we have to establish a most-powerful system that limits itself and provides limits for the rest of our activities. Long ago, Eric Drexler proposed an Active Shield. Others have proposed building an AI [Artificial Intelligence] to govern us—though they have not explained how to build internal limits into the AI. I have proposed creating a government of people who have accepted modifications to their biochemistry to limit some of their human impulses. All of these suggestions have problems.

Chris Phoenix, "The Need For Limits,"
Wise-nano.org, 2008. www.wise-nano.org.

and establishing dominance; 3) some other nation developing earlier and establishing dominance; 4) international cooperation and trust sufficient to ensure safety; 5) a multinational organization willing and able to keep the peace."

"Option 1 is undesirable; Option 3 is probably unthinkable for any of the current large powers; Option 5 is probably unacceptable to the U.S., as the world's sole superpower; Option 4 may be seen as unfeasible. Only one nation can succeed at Option 2. This implies that a preemptive strike option (whether military attack, or sabotage or derailment of nanotech development efforts) will appear very attractive to a number of powerful nations."

If Option 4 were feasible, then we would have world peace now. Option 5 is only feasible if the multinational organization in question is given sufficient authority and military power to disarm and regulate the nations of the world. By definition, this would be a global government.

So, essentially, once molecular manufacturing is developed, the developing nation has two options:

1. Conquer competing nations so as to prevent them from constructing a rival MM capability.

2. Given the available options, it should come as no surprise that world domination will win out.

The Inevitability of Global Government

Once the leading MM-enabled power uses its advantage to destroy the potential molecular manufacturing capability of suspected rivals, it will then face a much tougher decision: how to go about governing the world. The leading nation will need to institute some form of a global regulatory body to insure that molecular manufacturing does not fall into the wrong hands. Only two choices seem viable:

1. *Federalism*—a centralized governing authority that oversees the entire world population.

2. *Confederation*—a loosely associated collection of states who work together to administer world government.

Option 2 would still require a leading authority to maintain a monopoly on molecular manufacturing and extinguish any attempts to create a rival power—whether that power be a nation, a group, or an individual. As a result, both options inevitably lead to a centralized global government—a global government that must maintain constant vigilance toward the possible threat of an emerging power. This constant vigilance will require continuous global surveillance.

A Surveillance Society

Imagine a scenario in which a single individual in possession of unrestricted technology and resources could conquer the entire world. This will be our world in the era of molecular manufacturing. With such high stakes and an almost infinite number of potential threats, the world population will require some means of defense. And that defense will require around-the-clock, ever-present surveillance of the world at large.

A system of safeguards will have to be constructed in order to prevent emerging nation states, terrorist groups, and individuals from breaching the peace. A single global government will go a long way toward eliminating military conflict, as there will be only one military power with a unified purpose. However, in the era of molecular manufacturing, competing militaries could rise quickly, and to prevent a loss of its governing monopoly, a global government will have to deploy unprecedented measures.

This surveillance could be "god-like" in scope—seeing everything, hearing everything, and knowing everything. Imagine "nanodust"—nanoscale cameras and listening devices as plentiful and as difficult to remove as common, everyday dust. MM will enable the construction of trillions of these sophisticated devices at negligible cost.

Outfitted with advanced artificial intelligence software, these devices could sift through continuous video and audio feeds, searching for predetermined patterns indicative of what the state believes to be "aberrant" behavior. This isn't difficult to imagine. Similar pattern recognition technologies are already in widespread use. MM can simply extend these applications to encompass all speech and actions on the face of the earth.

With the need for constant vigilance against any potential emerging MM powers, global surveillance will have to be administered on some sort global level, meaning that a final global authority for resolving and enforcing international disputes must emerge. This is why global government is inevitable.

Biblical Prediction Means End of World

Okay, so global government is imminent and inevitable. What's the big deal, you ask? The reason this is such a big deal is revealed in the Bible. Centuries ago, the Bible predicted that a global government would arise in the last day. . . . And this global government will only appear on the world scene in parallel with the Antichrist, so we can't speculate that it will exist for an undetermined time period before he appears:

> "His ten horns are ten kings who have not yet risen to power; they will be appointed to their kingdoms for one brief moment to reign with the beast. They will all agree to give their power and authority to him."
>
> *Revelation 17:12–13*

Global government comes about as a direct result of ten kings freely providing their power and authority to a centralized global government. The establishment of this global government, and the rise of the Antichrist to administer it, is a monumental sign which heralds the soon return of Jesus Christ to establish His Kingdom on Earth.

"*Scientists are currently debating what discovery could set off a chain reaction of Earth-altering technological events. They suggest that advancements in the fields of nanotechnology or the discovery of artificial intelligence could usher in the Singularity.*"

Nanotechnology Will Contribute to a "Singularity"

James John Bell

In the following viewpoint, James Bell asserts that molecular nanotechnology will contribute to the occurrence of a technological "Singularity," an event of epic proportions which threatens the very existence of humans. Bell says that advances in computer technology, biotechnology, and nanotechnology are occurring at faster and faster rates. Eventually, he says, advances will occur so fast that machines will become more intelligent than humans. At this point, Bell and other scientists believe that the mass destruction of humans and the natural world is entirely possible. Bell is an author of science fiction and social change. He co-founded the nonprofit advocacy communications organization smartMeme in 2002.

James John Bell, "Exploring the Singularity," *The Futurist*, June 1, 2003. Copyright © 2003 James John Bell. Reproduced by permission of The World Future Society. www.kurzweilai.net.

As you read, consider the following questions:

1. According to Bell, which law did Stewart Brand discuss in his book, *The Clock of the Long Now*? What does this law state?

2. What does Bell call people who believe that unchecked technological progress will exceed human ability to reverse any destruction the technology may set in motion?

3. According to Bell, who coined the term "robot" and what does it mean in Czech?

Technological change isn't just happening fast. It's happening at an exponential rate. Contrary to the commonsense, intuitive, linear view, we won't just experience 100 years of progress in the twenty-first century—it will be more like 20,000 years of progress.

The near-future results of exponential technological growth will be staggering: the merging of biological and non-biological entities in bio-robotics, plants and animals engineered to grow pharmaceutical drugs, software-based "life," smart robots, and atom-sized machines that self-replicate like living matter. Some individuals are even warning that we could lose control of this expanding techno-cornucopia and cause the total extinction of life as we know it. Others are researching how this permanent technological overdrive will affect us. They're trying to understand what this new world of ours will look like and how accelerating technology already impacts us.

Perspectives of a "Singularity"

A number of scientists believe machine intelligence will surpass human intelligence within a few decades, leading to what's come to be called the Singularity. Author and inventor Ray Kurzweil defines this phenomenon as "technological change so rapid and profound it could create a rupture in the very fabric of human history."

Singularity is technically a mathematical term, perhaps best described as akin to what happens on world maps in a standard atlas. Everything appears correct until we look at regions very close to the poles. In the standard Mercator projection[1], the poles appear not as points but as a straight line. Each line is a singularity: Everywhere along the top line contains the exact point of the North Pole, and the bottom line is the entire South Pole.

The singularity on the edge of the map is nothing compared to the singularity at the center of a black hole. Here one finds the astrophysicist's singularity, a rift in the continuum of space and time where Einstein's rules no longer function. The approaching technological Singularity, like the singularities of black holes, marks a point of departure from reality. Explorers once wrote "Beyond here be dragons" on the edges of old maps of the known world, and the image of life as we approach these edges of change are proving to be just as mysterious, dangerous, and controversial.

There is no concise definition for the Singularity. Kurzweil and many transhumanists define it as "a future time when societal, scientific, and economic change is so fast we cannot even imagine what will happen from our present perspective." A range of dates is given for the advent of the Singularity. "I'd be surprised if it happened before 2004 or after 2030," writes author and computer science professor Vernor Vinge. A distinctive feature will be that machine intelligence will have exceeded and even merged with human intelligence. Another definition is used by extropians [those who advocate for using technology to extend the human life span], who say it denotes "the singular time when technological development will be at its fastest." From an environmental perspective, the Singularity can be thought of as the point at which technology and nature become one. Whatever perspective one takes, at this junc-

1. A map projection that attempts to fit a curved surface onto a flat sheet. Commonly used for ocean navigation.

ture the world as we have known it will become extinct, and new definitions of life, nature, and human will take hold.

Many leading technology industries have been aware of the possibility of a Singularity for some time. There are concerns that, if the public understood its ramifications, they might panic over accepting new and untested technologies that bring us closer to Singularity. For now, the debate about the consequences of the Singularity has stayed within the halls of business and technology; the kinks are being worked out, avoiding "doomsday" hysteria. At this time, it appears to matter little if the Singularity ever truly comes to pass.

What Will Singularity Look Like?

Kurzweil explains that central to the workings of the Singularity are a number of "laws," one of which is Moore's law. Intel cofounder Gordon E. Moore noted that the number of transistors that could fit on a single computer chip had doubled every year for six years from the beginnings of integrated circuits in 1959. Moore predicted that the trend would continue, and it has—although the doubling rate was later adjusted to an 18-month cycle.

Today, the smallest transistors in chips span only thousands of atoms (hundreds of nanometers). Chipmakers build such components using a process in which they apply semiconducting, metallic, and insulating layers to a semiconductor wafer to create microscopic circuitry. They accomplish the procedure using light for imprinting patterns onto the wafer. In order to keep Moore's law moving right along, researchers today have built circuits out of transistors, wires, and other components as tiny as a few atoms across that can carry out simple computations.

Kurzweil and Sun Microsystems' chief scientist Bill Joy agree that, circa 2030, the technology of the 1999 film *The Matrix* (which visualized a three-dimensional interface between humans and computers, calling conventional reality into question) will be within our grasp and that humanity will be teetering on the edge of the Singularity. Kurzweil explains that this will become possible because Moore's law will be replaced by another computing paradigm over the next few decades. "Moore's law was not the first but the fifth paradigm to provide exponential growth of computing power," Kurzweil says. The first paradigm of computer technology was the data processing machinery used in the 1890 American census. This electromechanical computing technology was followed by the paradigms of relay-based technology, vacuum tubes, transistors, and eventually integrated circuits. "Every time a paradigm ran out of steam," states Kurzweil, "another paradigm came along and picked up where that paradigm left off." The sixth paradigm, the one that will enable technology à la *The Matrix*, will be here in 20 to 30 years. "It's obvious what the sixth paradigm will be—computing in three dimensions," says Kurzweil. "We will effectively merge with our technology."

Stewart Brand in his book *The Clock of the Long Now* discusses the Singularity and another related law, Monsanto's law, which states that the ability to identify and use genetic information doubles every 12 to 24 months. This exponential growth in biological knowledge is transforming agriculture, nutrition, and health care in the emerging life-sciences industry.

A field of research building on the exponential growth rate of biotechnology is nanotechnology—the science of building machines out of atoms. A nanometer is atomic in scale, a distance that's 0.001% of the width of human hair. One goal of this science is to change the atomic fabric of matter—to engineer machinelike atomic structures that reproduce like living matter. In this respect, it is similar to biotechnology, except that nanotechnology needs to literally create something like an inorganic version of DNA to drive the building of its tiny machines. "We're working out the rules of biology in a realm where nature hasn't had the opportunity to work," states University of Texas biochemistry professor Angela Belcher. "What would take millions of years to evolve on its own takes about three weeks on the bench top."

Machine progress is knocking down the barriers between all the sciences. Chemists, biologists, engineers, and physicists are now finding themselves collaborating on more and more experimental research. This collaboration is best illustrated by the opening of Cornell University's Nanobiotechnology Center and other such facilities around the world. These scientists predict breakthroughs soon that will open the way to molecular-size computing and the quantum computer, creating new scientific paradigms where exponential technological progress will leap off the map. Those who have done the exponential math quickly realize the possibilities in numerous industries and scientific fields—and then they notice the anomaly of the Singularity happening within this century.

In 2005, IBM plans to introduce Blue Gene [As of December 2008, there were four Blue Gene computers in development], a supercomputer that can perform at about 5% of the power of the human brain. This computer could transmit the entire contents of the Library of Congress in less than two seconds. Blue Gene/L, specifically developed to advance and serve the growing life-sciences industry, is expected to operate at about 200 teraflops (200 trillion floating-point operations per second), larger than the total computing power of the top 500 supercomputers in the world. It will be able to run extremely complex simulations, including breakthroughs in computers and information technology, creating new frontiers in biology, says IBM's Paul M. Horn. According to Moore's law, computer hardware will surpass human brainpower in the first decade of this century. Software that emulates the human mind—artificial intelligence—may take another decade to evolve.

Nanotech Advances Promote Singularity

Physicists, mathematicians, and scientists like Vinge and Kurz-weil have identified through their research the likely boundaries of the Singularity and have predicted with confidence various paths leading up to it over the next couple of decades. These scientists are currently debating what discovery could set off a chain reaction of Earth-altering technological events. They suggest that advancements in the fields of nanotechnology or the discovery of artificial intelligence could usher in the Singularity.

The majority of people closest to these theories and laws—the tech sector—can hardly wait for these technologies to arrive. The true believers call themselves extropians, posthumans, and transhumanists, and are actively organizing not just to bring the Singularity about, but to counter the technophobes and neo-Luddites [Luddites were a group of artisans protesting the automation of the Industrial Revolution] who believe that unchecked technological progress will exceed our ability to reverse any destructive process that might unintentionally be set in motion.

The antithesis to neo-Luddite activists is the extropians. For example, the Progress Action Coalition, formed in 2001 by bio-artist, author, and extropian activist Natasha Vita-More, fantasizes about "the dream of true artificial intelligence . . . adding a new richness to the human landscape never before known." Pro-Act, AgBioworld, Biotechnology Progress, Foresight Institute, the Progress and Freedom Foundation, and other industry groups acknowledge, however, that the greatest threat to technological progress comes not just from environmental groups, but from a small faction of the scientific community.

Knowledge-Enabled Mass Destruction

In April 2000, a wrench was thrown into the arrival of the Singularity by an unlikely source: Sun Microsystems chief scientist Bill Joy. He is a neo-Luddite without being a Luddite, a technologist warning the world about technology. Joy co-founded Sun Microsystems, helped create the Unix computer operating system, and developed the Java and Jini software systems—systems that helped give the Internet "life."

In a now-infamous cover story in *Wired* magazine, "Why the Future Doesn't Need Us," Joy warned of the dangers posed by developments in genetics, nanotechnology, and robotics. Joy's warning of the impacts of exponential technological progress run amok gave new credence to the coming Singularity. Unless things change, Joy predicted, "We could be the last generation of humans." Joy warned that "knowledge alone will enable mass destruction" and termed this phenomenon "knowledge-enabled mass destruction."

The twentieth century gave rise to nuclear, biological, and chemical (NBC) technologies that, while powerful, require access to vast amounts of raw (and often rare) materials, technical information, and large-scale industries. The twenty-first-century technologies of genetics, nanotechnology, and robotics (GNR), however, will require neither large facilities nor rare raw materials.

The threat posed by GNR technologies becomes further amplified by the fact that some of these new technologies have been designed to be able to replicate—i.e., they can build new versions of themselves. Nuclear bombs did not sprout more bombs, and toxic spills did not grow more spills. If the new self-replicating GNR technologies are released into the environment, they could be nearly impossible to recall or control.

Joy understands that the greatest dangers we face ultimately stem from a world where global corporations dominate—a future where much of the world has no voice in how the world is run. Twenty-first-century GNR technologies, he writes, "are being developed almost exclusively by corporate enterprises. We are aggressively pursuing the promises of these new technologies within the now-unchallenged system of global capitalism and its manifold financial incentives and competitive pressures."

Joy believes that the system of global capitalism, combined with our current rate of progress, gives the human race a 30% to 50% chance of going extinct around the time the Singularity is expected to happen, around 2030. "Not only are these estimates not encouraging," he adds, "but they do not include the probability of many horrid outcomes that lie short of extinction."

It is very likely that scientists and global corporations will miss key developments—or, worse, actively avoid discussion of them. A whole generation of biologists has left the field for the biotech and nanotech labs. Biologist Craig Holdredge, who has followed biotech since its beginnings in the 1970s, warns, "Biology is losing its connection with nature."

When Machines Make War

Cloning, biotechnology, nanotechnology, and robotics are blurring the lines between nature and machine. In his 1972 speech "The Android and the Human," science-fiction visionary Philip K. Dick told his audience, "Machines are becoming more human. Our environment, and I mean our man-made world of machines, is becoming alive in ways specifically and fundamentally analogous to ourselves." In the near future, Dick prophesied, a human might shoot a robot only to see it bleed from its wound. When the robot shoots back, it may be surprised to find the human gush smoke. "It would be rather a great moment of truth for both of them," Dick added.

In November 2001, Advanced Cell Technology of Massachusetts jarred the nation's focus away from recession and terrorism when it announced that it had succeeded in cloning early-stage human embryos. Debate on the topic stayed equally

The Singularity, Of Course

What else would you call it . . .

- When we start using nanotechnology to repair bodies at the cellular level?

- When catching up on the latest research is a mere matter of *desiring* information, whereupon autonomous software agents deliver it to you, as quickly and easily as your arm now moves wherever you wish it to?

- When on-demand production becomes so trivial that wealth and poverty become almost meaningless terms?

- When the virtual reality experience—say visiting a far-away planet—gets hard to distinguish from the real thing?

- When each of us can have as many "servants"—either robotic or software-based—as we like, as loyal as your own right hand?

- When augmented human intelligence will soar and—trading insights with one another at light speed—helping us attain entirely new levels of thought?

David Brin, "Singularities and Nightmares,"
Nanotechnology Perceptions, *March 27, 2006.*

divided between those who support therapeutic cloning and those, like the American Medical Association, who want an outright ban.

Karel Capek coined the word robot (Czech for "forced labor") in the 1920 play *R.U.R.*, in which machines assume the drudgery of factory production, then develop feelings and proceed to wipe out humanity in a violent revolution. While the robots in *R.U.R.* could represent the "nightmare vision of the proletariat seen through middle-class eyes," as science-fiction author Thomas Disch has suggested, they also are testament to the persistent fears of man-made technology run amok.

Similar themes have manifested themselves in popular culture and folklore since at least medieval times. While some might dismiss these stories simply as popular paranoia, robots are already being deployed beyond Hollywood and are poised to take over the deadlier duties of the modern soldier. The Pentagon is replacing soldiers with sensors, vehicles, aircraft, and weapons that can be operated by remote control or are autonomous. Pilotless aircraft played an important role in the bombings of Afghanistan, and a model called the Gnat conducted surveillance flights in the Philippines in 2002.

Leading the Pentagon's remote-control warfare effort is the Defense Advanced Research Projects Agency (DARPA). Best known for creating the infrastructure that became the World Wide Web, DARPA is working with Boeing to develop the X-45 unmanned combat air vehicle. The 30-foot-long windowless planes will carry up to 12 bombs, each weighing 250 pounds. According to military analysts, the X-45 will be used to attack radar and antiaircraft installations as early as 2007. By 2010, it will be programmed to distinguish friends from foes without consulting humans and independently attack targets in designated areas. By 2020, robotic planes and vehicles will direct remote-controlled bombers toward targets, robotic helicopters will coordinate driverless convoys, and unmanned submarines will clear mines and launch cruise missiles.

Rising to the challenge of mixing man and machine, MIT's [Massachusetts Institute of Technology's] Institute for Soldier Nanotechnologies (backed by a five-year, $50-million U.S. Army grant) is busy innovating materials and designs to create military uniforms that rival the best science fiction. Human soldiers themselves are being transformed into modern cyborgs through robotic devices and nanotechnology.

The Biorobotic Arms Race

The 2002 International Conference on Robotics and Automation, hosted by the Institute of Electrical and Electronics Engineers, kicked off its technical session with a discussion on biorobots, the melding of living and artificial structures into a cybernetic organism or cyborg.

"In the past few years, the biosciences and robotics have been getting closer and closer," says Paolo Dario, founder of Italy's Advanced Robotics Technology and Systems Lab. "More and more, biological models are used for the design of biometric robots [and] robots are increasingly used by neuroscientists as clinical platforms for validating biological models." Artificial constructs are beginning to approach the scale and complexity of living systems.

Shocking Realities

Some of the scientific breakthroughs expected in the next few years promise to make cloning and robotics seem rather benign. The merging of technology and nature has already yielded some shocking progeny. Consider these examples:

- Researchers at the State University of New York Health Science Center at Brooklyn have turned a living rat into a radio-controlled automaton using three electrodes placed in the animal's brain. The animal can be remotely steered through an obstacle course, making it twist, turn, and jump on demand.

- In May 2002, eight elderly Florida residents were injected with microscopic silicon identification chips encoded with medical information. *The Los Angeles Times* reported that this made them "scannable just like a jar of peanut butter in the supermarket checkout line."

Applied Digital Solutions Inc., the maker of the chip, will soon have a prototype of an implantable device able to receive GPS satellite signals and transmit a person's location.

- Human embryos have been successfully implanted and grown in artificial wombs. The experiments were halted after a few days to avoid violating in vitro fertilization regulations.

- Researchers in Israel have fashioned a "bio-computer" out of DNA that can handle a billion operations per second with 99.8% accuracy. Reuters reports that these bio-computers are so minute that "a trillion of them could fit inside a test tube."

- In England, University of Reading Professor Kevin Warwick has implanted microchips in his body to remotely monitor and control his physical motions. During Warwick's Project Cyborg experiments, computers were able to remotely monitor his movements and open doors at his approach.

- Engineers at the U.S. Sandia National Labs have built a remote-controlled spy robot equipped with a scanner, microphone, and chemical microsensor. The robot weighs one ounce and is smaller than a dime. Lab scientists predict that the microbot could prove invaluable in protecting U.S. military and economic interests.

The next arms race is not based on replicating and perfecting a single deadly technology, like the nuclear bombs of the past or some space-based weapon of the future. This new arms race is about accelerating the development and integration of advanced autonomous, biotechnological, and human-robotic systems into the military apparatus. A mishap or a massive war using these new technologies could be more catastrophic than any nuclear war.

Where the Map Exceeds the Territory

The rate at which GNR technologies are being adopted by our society—without regard to long-term safety testing or researching the political, cultural, and economic ramifications—mirrors the development and proliferation of nuclear power and weapons. The human loss caused by experimentation, production, and development is still being felt from the era of NBC technologies.

The discussion of the environmental impacts of GNR technologies, at least in the United States, has been relegated to the margins. Voices of concern and opposition have likewise been missing in discussions of the technological Singularity. The true cost of this technological progress and any coming Singularity will mean the unprecedented decline of the planet's inhabitants at an ever-increasing rate of global extinction.

Nature and Technology, Competing and Combining

The World Conservation Union, the International Botanical Congress, and a majority of the world's biologists believe that a global mass extinction already is under way. As a direct result of human activity (resource extraction, industrial agriculture, the introduction of non-native animals, and population growth), up to one-fifth of all living species are expected to disappear within 30 years. A 1998 Harris Poll of the 5,000 members of the American Institute of Biological Sciences found that 70% believed that what has been termed "The Sixth Extinction" is now under way. A simultaneous Harris Poll found that 60% of the public were totally unaware of the impending biological collapse.

At the same time that nature's ancient biological creation is on the decline, laboratory-created biotech life-forms—genetically modified soybeans, genetically engineered salmon, cloned sheep, drug-crops, biorobots—are on the rise.

149

Nature and technology are not just evolving; they are competing and combining with one another. Ultimately they will become one. We hear reports daily about these new technologies and new creations, while shreds of the ongoing biological collapse surface here and there. Past the edges of change, beyond the wall across the future, anything becomes possible. Beware the dragons.

VIEWPOINT

"*I can't take seriously the predictions that life-altering molecular nanotechnology will arrive within 15 or 20 years and hasten the arrival of a technological singularity before 2050.*"

Nanotechnology Will Not Contribute to a "Singularity"

Richard Jones

In the following viewpoint, Richard Jones maintains that a nanoenabled singularity is more fantasy than fact. Jones asserts that people who believe that nanotechnology will one day lead to a technological singularity—where technology advances so fast that humans become extinct and cyborgs rule the earth—are underestimating the enormous challenges of creating nanoscale assemblers. One of the primary rationales behind the feasibility of nanoscale assemblers is that nature has already created them in the form of biological cells. According to Jones, making nanomachines out of rigid materials like steel is vastly different than

---

making nanomachines out of the soft and wet materials that comprise biological cells.

what goes on in biological cells. Jones sees several other practical problems with nanomachines that put the idea of a singularity in serious doubt. Jones is a professor of physics at the University of Sheffield in England and a nanotechnology advisor to the British government.

As you read, consider the following questions:

1. According to Jones, the difference between a singularity vision and today's research is a bit like the gap between what two modes of transportation?

2. According to Jones, which cellular molecule is the stickiest of all?

3. What does Jones believe might be the real killer application for the idea of software controlled matter?

How to usher humanity into an era of transhumanist bliss: first, end scarcity. Second, eradicate death. Third, eliminate the bungled mechanisms that introduce imperfections into the human body. The vehicle for accomplishing all three? Molecular nanotechnology—in essence, the reduction of all material things to the status of software.

To reduce the splendid complexity of our world to a list of instructions, a mere recipe, would involve harnessing the most basic components of life. Start with Earth's supply of atoms. Evolution, the laws of physics, and a big dose of chance have arranged those atoms into the objects and life-forms around us. If we could map the position and type of every atom in an object and also place atoms in specific positions, then in principle we could reproduce with absolute fidelity any material thing from its constituent parts. At a stroke, any material or artifact—a Stradivarius [violin] or a steak—could be available in abundance. We could build replacement body parts with capabilities that would hugely exceed their natural analogues. The economy, the environment, even what it means to be human, would be utterly transformed.

Anticipating a Singularity? Don't Hold Your Breath

This vision holds wide currency among those anticipating a singularity, in which the creation of hyperintelligent, self-replicating machines triggers runaway technological advancement and economic growth, transforming human beings into cyborgs that are superhuman and maybe even immortal. Some of these futurists are convinced that this renaissance is just a few decades away. But in academia and industry, nanotechnologists are working on a very different set of technologies. Many of these projects will almost certainly prove to be useful, lucrative, or even transformative, but none of them is likely to bring about the transhumanist rapture foreseen by singularitarians. Not in the next century, anyway.

It's not that the singularity vision is completely unrecognizable in today's work. It's just that the gulf between the two is a bit like the gap between traveling by horse and buggy and by interplanetary transport. The birth of nanotechnology is popularly taken to be 1989, when IBM Fellow Don Eigler used a scanning tunneling microscope to create the company's logo out of xenon atoms. Since then a whole field has emerged, based mainly on custom-engineered molecules that have gone into such consumer items as wrinkle-free clothes, more-effective sunscreens, and sturdier sports rackets.

However, it is a very long way indeed from a top-notch tennis racket to smart nanoscale robots capable of swarming in our bodies like infinitesimal guardian angels, recognizing and fixing damaged cells or DNA, and detecting, chasing, and destroying harmful viruses and bacteria. But the transhumanists underestimate the magnitude of that leap. They look beyond the manipulation of an atom or molecule with a scanning tunneling microscope and see swarms of manipulators that are themselves nanoscale. Under software control, these "nanofactories" would be able to arrange atoms in any pattern consistent with the laws of physics.

Rather than simply copying existing materials, the transhumanists dream of integrating into those materials almost unlimited functionality: state-of-the-art sensing and information processing could be built into the very fabric of our existence, accompanied by motors with astounding power density. Singularitarians anticipate that Moore's Law [the trend of computing technologies to increase exponentially over time] will run on indefinitely, giving us the immense computing power in tiny packages needed to control these nanofactories. These minuscule robots, or nanobots, need not be confined to protecting our bodies, either: if they can fix and purify, why not extend and enhance? Neural nanobots could allow a direct interface between our biological wetware and powerful computers with vast databases.

Maybe we could leave our bodies entirely. Only the need to preserve the contents of our memories and consciousness, our mental identities, ties us to them. Perhaps those nanobots will even be able to swim through our brains to read and upload our thoughts and memories, indeed entire personalities, to a powerful computer.

Drexler's Vision

This expansive view of molecular nanotechnology owes as much to K. Eric Drexler as to anyone else. A MIT [Massachusetts Institute of Technology] graduate and student of Marvin Minsky, Drexler laid out his vision in the 1992 book *Nanosystems*. Those ideas have been picked up and expanded by other futurists over the past 16 years.

In his book, Drexler envisaged nanostructures built from the strongest and stiffest materials available, using the rational design principles of mechanical engineering. The fundamental building blocks of this paradigm are tiny, rigid cogs and gears, analogous to the plastic pieces of a Lego set. The gears would distribute power from nanoscale electric motors and be small enough to assist in the task of attaching molecules to one another. They would also process information. Drexler drew inspiration from a previous generation of computing devices, which used levers and gears rather than transistors, for his vision of ultrasmall mechanical computers.

Assuming that an object's structure could easily be reduced to its molecular blueprint, the first order of business is figuring out how to translate macroscale manufacturing methods into nanoscale manipulations. For example, let's say you wanted a new pancreas. Your first major challenge stems from the fact that a single human cell is composed of about 1014 atoms, and the pancreas you want has at least 80 billion cells, probably more. We could use a scanning tunneling microscope to position individual atoms with some precision, but to make a macroscopic object with it would take a very long time.

The theoretical solution, initially, was an idea known as exponential manufacturing. In its simplest form, this refers to a hypothetical nanoscale "assembler" that could construct objects on its own scale. For instance, it could make another assembler, and each assembler could go on to make more assemblers, resulting in a suite of assemblers that would combine forces to make a macroscopic object.

Setting aside the enormous challenges of creating and coordinating these nanoassemblers, some theorists have worried about a doomsday scenario known as the "gray goo" problem. Runaway replicators could voraciously consume resources to produce ever more stuff, a futuristic take on the old story of the sorcerer's apprentice. Not to worry, say Drexler and colleagues. In the latest vision of the nanofactory, the reproducing replicators give way to Henry Ford-style mass production, with endlessly repeated elementary operations on countless tiny production lines.

Humans Are Full of Nanoassemblers

It's a seductive idea, seemingly validated by the workings of the cells of our own bodies. We're full of sophisticated nanoassemblers: delve into the inner workings of a typical cell and you'll find molecular motors that convert chemical energy into mechanical energy and membranes with active ion channels that sort molecules—two key tasks needed for basic nanoscale assembly. ATP synthase, for example, is an intricate cluster of proteins constituting a mechanism that makes adenosine triphosphate, the molecule that fuels the contraction of muscle cells and countless other cellular processes. Cell biology also exhibits software-controlled manufacturing, in the form of protein synthesis. The process starts with the ribosome, a remarkable molecular machine that can read information from a strand of messenger RNA and convert the code into a sequence of amino acids. The amino-acid sequence in turn defines the three-dimensional structure of a protein and its function. The ribosome fulfils the functions expected of an artificial assembler—proof that complex nanoassembly is possible.

If biology can produce a sophisticated nanotechnology based on soft materials like proteins and lipids, singularitarian thinking goes, then how much more powerful our synthetic nanotechnology would be if we could use strong, stiff materials, like diamond. And if biology can produce working motors and assemblers using just the random selections of Darwinian evolution, how much more powerful the devices could be if they were rationally designed using all the insights we've learned from macroscopic engineering.

Mimicking Cell Biology to Make Nanomachines Is Doubtful

But that reasoning fails to take into account the physical environment in which cell biology takes place, which has nothing in common with the macroscopic world of bridges, engines, and transmissions. In the domain of the cell, water behaves like thick molasses, not the free-flowing liquid that we are familiar with. This is a world dominated by the fluctuations of constant Brownian motion, in which components are ceaselessly bombarded by fast-moving water molecules and flex and stretch randomly. The van der Waals force, which attracts molecules to one another, dominates, causing things in close proximity to stick together. Clingiest of all are protein molecules, whose stickiness underlies a number of undesirable phenomena, such as the rejection of medical implants. What's to protect a nanobot assailed by particles glomming onto its surface and clogging up its gears?

The watery nanoscale environment of cell biology seems so hostile to engineering that the fact that biology works at all is almost hard to believe. But biology does work—and very well at that. The lack of rigidity, excessive stickiness, and constant random motion may seem like huge obstacles to be worked around, but biology is aided by its own design principles, which have evolved over billions of years to exploit those characteristics. That brutal combination of strong surface forces and random Brownian motion in fact propels the self-assembly of sophisticated structures, such as the sculpting of intricately folded protein molecules. The cellular environment that at first seems annoying—filled with squishy objects and the chaotic banging around of particles—is essential in the operation of molecular motors, where a change in a protein molecule's shape provides the power stroke to convert chemical energy to mechanical energy.

In the end, rather than ratifying the "hard" nanomachine paradigm, cellular biology casts doubt on it. But even if that mechanical-engineering approach were to work in the body, there are several issues that, in my view, have been seriously underestimated by its proponents.

Several Practical Problems

First, those building blocks—the cogs and gears made famous in countless simulations supporting the case for the singularity—have some questionable chemical properties. They are es-

Questions to Ponder About a Technological Decline

The rate of innovation reached a peak over a hundred years ago and is now in decline. This decline is most likely due to an economic limit of technology or a limit of the human brain that we are approaching. We are now approximately 85% of the way to this limit, and the pace of technological development will diminish with each passing year. These conclusions are controversial, but there are profound implications if they are true, and the following questions are included for the interested reader to ponder:

- What are the implications for the economy, government and society of declining rates of innovation?

- What standard of living corresponds to the economic limit of technology?

- Will the level of technology reach a maximum and then decline as in the Dark Ages?

- Are there any key inventions that could reverse the current decline in the rate of innovation?

- Are there any other reasons for the decline in the rate of innovation during the 20th century besides the approach of an economic limit of technology or a limit of the human brain?

- What is the relationship between innovation and democracy?

Jonathan Huebner,
"A Possible Declining Trend for Worldwide Innovation,"
Technological Forecasting and Social Change, *2005.*

sentially molecular clusters with odd and special shapes, but it's far from clear that they represent stable arrangements of atoms that won't rearrange themselves spontaneously. These crystal lattices were designed using molecular modeling software, which works on the principle that if valences are satisfied and bonds aren't too distorted from their normal values, then the structures formed will be chemically stable. But this is a problematic assumption.

A regular crystal lattice is a 3-D arrangement of atoms or molecules with well-defined angles between the bonds that hold them together. To build a crystal lattice in a nonnatural shape—say, with a curved surface rather than with the flat faces characteristic of crystals—the natural distances and angles between atoms need to be distorted, severely straining those bonds. Modeling software might tell you that the bonds will hold. However, life has a way of confounding computer models. For example, if you try to make very small, spherical diamond crystals, a layer or two of carbon atoms at the surface will spontaneously rearrange themselves into a new form—not of diamond, but of graphite.

A second problem has to do with the power of surface forces and the high surface area anticipated for these nanobots. Researchers attempting to shrink existing microelectromechanical systems to the nanoscale have already discovered that the combination of friction and persistent sticking can be devastating. Nanobots are expected to operate at very high power densities, so even rather low values of friction may vaporize or burn up the minuscule machines. At the very least, this friction and sticking will play havoc with the machines' chemical stability.

Then there's the prospect of irreversible damage if reactive substances—such as water or oxygen—get caught up in a nanobot's exposed surfaces, upsetting the careful chemistry of each. To avoid those molecules, nanodevices will have to be fabricated in a fully controlled environment. No one yet knows how a medical nanobot would be protected once it is released into the warm, crowded turbulence of the body, perhaps the most heterogeneous environment imaginable.

Finally, there's the question of how an intricate arrangement of cogs and gears that depends on precision and rigidity to work will respond to thermal noise and Brownian bombardment at room temperature. The turbulence that nanobots will be subjected to will far exceed that inflicted on macroscopically engineered structures, and even the most rigid materials, like diamond, will bend and wobble in response. It would be like making a clock and its gears out of rubber, then watching it tumble around in a clothes dryer and wondering why it doesn't keep time. The bottom line is that we have no idea whether complex and rigid mechanical systems—even ones made from diamond—can survive in the nanoworld.

Put all these complications together and what they suggest, to me, is that the range of environments in which rigid nanomachines could operate, if they operate at all, would be quite limited. If, for example, such devices can function only at low temperatures and in a vacuum, their impact and economic importance would be virtually nil.

Not Even Close

In 15 years of intense nanotechnology research, we have not even come close to experiencing the exponentially accelerating technological progress toward the goals set out by singularitarians. Impressive advances are emerging from the labs of real-world nanotechnologists, but these have little to do with the Drexlerian vision, which seems to be accumulating obstacles faster than it can overcome them. Given these facts, I can't take seriously the predictions that life-altering molecular nanotechnology will arrive within 15 or 20 years and hasten the arrival of a technological singularity before 2050.

Rather than try to defy or resist nature, I say we need to work with it. DNA itself can be used as a construction material. We can exploit its astounding properties of self-assembly to make programmed structures to execute new and beneficial functions. Chemists have already made nanoscale molecular shuttles and motors inspired directly by biology, with exciting applications in drug delivery and tissue engineering.

We will reap major medical advances by radically reengineering existing microorganisms, especially in nanodevices that perform integrated diagnosis and treatment of some disorders. But the timescales to reach the clinic are going to be long, and the goal of cell-by-cell repair is far, far beyond our incomplete grasp of biological complexity.

Much the same can be said about the singularitarian computers that are needed to generate a complete reading of a mental state and brain implants that seamlessly integrate our thought processes with a computer network. True, brain-interface systems have already been built. A state-of-the-art system can read about 128 neurons. So: 128 down, 20 billion or so to go.

Nonetheless, I'm an optimist. I think that in the near future we'll successfully apply nanotechnology to the most pressing social challenges, such as energy and the environment. For example, new polymer- and nanoparticle-based photovoltaics may soon lead to dramatic improvements in the price and production of solar cells.

Less Radical, More Realistic Nanotech Goals

What, then, of software-controlled matter? Complete control will remain an unattainable goal for generations to come. But some combination of self-assembly and directed assembly could very well lead to precisely built nanostructures that would manipulate the way light, matter, and electrons interact—an application of nanotechnology that's already leading to exciting new discoveries. We've barely scratched the surface of what we'll eventually be able to do with these custom-built nanostructures. It is altogether possible that we will finally harness the unfamiliar quantum effects of the nanoscale to implement true quantum computing and information processing. Here, I suspect, is the true killer application for the idea of software-controlled matter: devices that integrate electronics and optics, fully exploiting their quantum character in truly novel ways—a far cry from the minuscule diamond engines foreseen by the transhumanists.

We shouldn't abandon all of the more radical goals of nanotechnology, because they may instead be achieved ultimately by routes quite different from (and longer than) those foreseen by the proponents of molecular nanotechnology. Perhaps we should thank Drexler for alerting us to the general possibilities of nanotechnology, while recognizing that the trajectories of new technologies rarely run smoothly along the paths foreseen by their pioneers.

Periodical Bibliography

The following articles have been selected to supplement the diverse views presented in this chapter.

Robert Adler "Entering a Dark Age of Innovation," *New Scientist.* July 2, 2005. www.newscientist.com.

James Cascio "Openness and the Metaverse Singularity," *KurzweilAI.net,* 2007. www.kurzweilai.net.

Peter Montague "Welcome to NanoWorld Nanotechnology and the Precautionary Principle," *The Multinational Monitor,* September 2004.

Andrew Moore "Waiter, There's a Nanobot in My Martini!" *European Molecular Biology Organization (EMBO) Reports,* May 2004.

Christine Peterson "Nanotechnology: From Feynman to the Grand Challenge of Molecular Manufacturing," *IEEE Technology and Society Magazine,* Winter 2004.

Charles T. Rubin "The Rhetoric of Extinction," *The New Atlantis,* Winter 2006.

Anthony Seaton and Kenneth Donaldson "Nanoscience, Nanotoxicology, and the Need to Think Small," *The Lancet,* March 12, 2005.

Michelle van Roost "The Coming Revolution in Molecular Manufacturing: Nanofiction or Nanotopia?" *Food Engineering & Ingredients,* February 2005.

Austin Weber "Nanotech Frontiers: Molecular Manufacturing Promises to Change the Way Many Products Are Assembled," *Assembly,* October 2004.

Rick Weiss "For Science, Nanotech Poses Big Unknowns," *Washington Post,* January 31, 2004.

Gary Wolf "Futurist Ray Kurzweil Pulls Out All the Stops (and Pills) to Live to Witness the Singularity," *Wired,* March 24, 2008. www.wired.com.

CHAPTER 3

What Are the Implications of Nanomedicine?

Chapter Preface

In a cement building about sixty miles southwest of Detroit, nearly one hundred cryopreserved patients are being kept in suspended animation. In November 2008, the ninety-first patient of the institute passed away. After paying $28,000, the sixty-five-year-old California man's body was flown to Detroit and sent immediately to the Cryonics Institute's facilities. Once at the institute, the man's body was carefully cryopreserved using antifreeze solutions and cooling to temperatures about two hundred degrees below freezing (about −196°C) with liquid nitrogen. The man is called a patient because the institute does not consider that he is irreversibly dead. They are preserving his organs and tissues for a future time when science may restore them to a viable state. Some people have only their heads frozen while others, like patient ninety-one, have their entire body cryopreserved. Many people believe that nanotechnology will make it possible to repair and revive the patients waiting in suspended animation at the Cryonics Institute. Many scientists, however, view cryonics and nanotechnology with skepticism.

The idea to freeze recently deceased people until science finds a way to defeat death was introduced to the public in the 1960s by Robert Ettinger, a Michigan physics teacher. Ettinger had been thinking about freezing to achieve immortality ever since the 1940s when he read about French biologist Dr. Jean Rostand's work freezing and then reviving frog sperm. Ettinger was intrigued with Rostand's speculation that someday the aged and infirm might be similarly treated and revived. Ettinger put his ideas into writing with the 1964 publication of *The Prospect of Immortality*. The book, which is often referred to as the bible of the cryonics movement, has been published in nine languages. In January 1967, retired psychology professor Dr. James Bedford became the first human being to be placed in cryonic suspension. Speaking about Bedford, himself, and others who are or will be placed in liquid nitrogen, Ettinger has said, "we already have made our arrangements for cryostasis after clinical death, signed our contracts with existing organizations and allocated the money. We will have our chance, and with a little bit of luck will 'taste the wine' of centuries unborn."

Many people believe that the key to cryonics' success lies with nanotechnology. Chapter nine of Eric Drexler's famous 1986 book, *Engines of Creation*, discusses how nanotechnology could be used to revive a patient who died of a heart attack and who was then frozen in liquid nitrogen:

Small devices examine molecules and report their structures and positions to a larger computer within the cell. The computer identifies the molecules, directs any needed molecular repairs, and identifies cell structures from molecular patterns. Where damage has displaced structures in a cell, the computer directs the repair devices to restore the molecules to their proper arrangement, using temporary cross-links as needed. Meanwhile, the patient's arteries are cleared and the heart muscle, damaged years earlier, is repaired ... heartbeat resumes, and the patient emerges into a state of anesthesia. While the attending physicians check that all is going well, the repair system closes the opening in the chest, joining tissue to tissue without a stitch or a scar. The remaining devices in the cells disassemble one another into harmless waste or nutrient molecules. As the patient moves into ordinary sleep, certain visitors enter the room, as long planned.

At last, the sleeper wakes refreshed to the light of a new day—and to the sight of old friends.

Drexler provided details to what had previously been only a concept. He described exactly how a patient suspended in liquid nitrogen might be revived at some future date: Nanorobots injected into the frozen patient would repair damaged cells and rejuvenate the patient to new life.

While cryonicists, such as Ettinger, are elated with Drexler's depiction of nano-enabled cryonics. Other scientists are highly skeptical. Michael Schermer, executive director of the Skeptics Society, is an outspoken critic of nanocryonics. He thinks the odds that the frozen patients at the Cryonics Institute will ever be revived is only slightly better than zero. In a 2001 *Scientific American* article Schermer expresses his skepticism, "This is what I call 'borderlands science,' because it dwells in that fuzzy region of claims that have yet to pass any tests but have some basis, however remote, in reality. It is not impossible for cryonics to succeed; it is just exceptionally unlikely."

To Ettinger, cryonicists, and others, nanotechnology provides the hope of future immortality. They believe the day will come when nanotechnology can cure disease, reverse injuries, and defeat death. Others like Schermer, however, believe that cryonics and nanorobots floating around the human body and fixing damaged cells are more fiction than reality. In the following chapter, scientists and others, debate the future role of nanotechnology in medicine and its implications for humanity.

| *"Nanomedicine will be one of the greatest boons in human history."*

Nanotechnology Will Revolutionize Medicine

Alan H. Goldstein

In the following viewpoint, Alan H. Goldstein claims that nanotechnology will dramatically transform the field of medicine in the not too distant future. Goldstein depicts what a future doctor's exam room might look like and describes how nanotech devices will be used to detect, analyze, and kill a cancerous cell the moment it arises. Goldstein thinks that eventually medicine will no longer be based on a one-size fits all approach—future medical treatments will be precisely individualized based on a person's genetic makeup. According to Goldstein, the changes brought about by nanomedicine will carry with them a wide range of new ethical questions regarding the delivery of health care around the world. Alan H. Goldstein is a nanobiotechnology research scientist and futurist.

As you read, consider the following questions:

1. What is the name of the technique that Goldstein says allows a single cancer cell among millions of healthy cells to be "hooked" and "reeled in" like a fish?

2. What are microbivores, according to the artist who depicted them in illustrations at the Nanomedicine Art Gallery?

3. According to Goldstein, what field is receiving almost universal acclaim as a worthy goal for the future of medicine? What field does Goldstein imply has not had universal acclaim?

It's the not-too-distant future, say 2016. You have been diagnosed with Stage III melanoma. Cancer has metastasized throughout your body. Just 10 years ago, in 2006, the choice of treatment would have been based on the type of primary cancer, the size and location of the metastasis, your age, your general health and your treatment history. Your prognosis would have been gloomy. But that was back in 2006, before we entered the era of nanomedicine.

A Rainbow of Nanomedicine Paraphernalia

In 2016, your doctor will be capable of scanning your entire genome in a few minutes. She will do this because every cell has a different gene expression pattern or profile. When a cell becomes cancerous, this profile changes. Your Stage III melanoma has a unique, schizoid genetic signature reflecting both a skin cell heritage and a newly acquired outlaw metabolism. Your doctor will explain that while your cancer has a great deal in common with other Stage III melanomas, it is not exactly like any other. Your doctor knows this because for the past few years DNA from virtually every melanoma patient in the U.S. health care system has been routinely extracted, scanned and deposited in a national database. This population of sequences, fully analyzed and with a user-friendly graphic interface, is available in real time. Searching this database for any specific cancer sequence will be about as difficult in 2016 as finding Madonna's birthday on Google is today.

The exam room of 2016 reflects a rainbow of nanomedicine paraphernalia. Diaphanous [delicate] pink microtubes sit in bubble packs like sets of false nails. Red motorized pipettes [glass tubes] hang in translucent blue plastic racks like designer tool kits from the Starship Enterprise. Shelves are filled with what appear to be airline-size single-serving cereal boxes with very slick, stunningly bright labeling. These boxes contain individually packaged, ready-to-use diagnostic kits with exciting brand names—DNA Warrior, Mighty Clone or Gene Catcher. An invisibly small drop of your body's fluid is injected into the DNA Warrior, which is a cylindrical cassette the size of a pinhead. This cassette is slotted into the Sherlock Genomes molecular diagnostics system.

From the outside, this "system" appears considerably less complex than your current cellular telephone. Inside, a single melanoma cell is purified from your blood via solid-phase fluorescent immunoaffinity chromatography, a technique in which a single cancer cell is "hooked" from amid millions of its healthy companions using a synthetic antibody molecule and "reeled in" on the beam of light produced when the two unite. Twenty years ago this technique required a million-dollar instrument the size of a 767 cockpit and a dedicated operator. Now it is little more than routine blood work.

Once purified, the renegade cell is moved via electroosmotic microfluidic channels to a lab chip that, in another venue, could pass for a credit card. Electroosmosis uses the charged molecules on the surface of the channel itself to cause a solution to flow in a specific direction. This will only work when a tube or channel is extremely small. Microfluidics use pipes the size of a human hair to create plumbing systems that empty into reaction chambers much smaller than the head of a pin. This enormous volume is dictated by the dimensions of your humanity—any smaller and a living cell wouldn't fit inside. On the lab chip, a purified cancer cell relinquishes its cache of chromosomes and within seconds your entire genome has been sequenced. That bears repeating. In a few years single-molecule DNA sequencing will be a reality. The 2.91 billion bits of biological data that bestow your unique genetic identity will be available virtually anytime for the cost of a routine blood test. Sound far-fetched? Two weeks ago J. Craig Venter, the genomics entrepreneur who paced the U.S. government to the completion of the Human Genome Project, announced that he hopes to offer $10 million as a prize (he originally pledged $500,000) for automated DNA sequencing technology that can decode a human genome for $1,000. At that same conference, a commercial instrument capable of sequencing 1 billion bases, or chemical groups, of DNA per day was unveiled.

A machine that "shreds" a billion bases of DNA a day could burn through the human genome in 72 hours. Yet we fully expect that this phenomenal accomplishment will be eclipsed within a few years by nanoengineering. Around the world, research teams are closing in on single-molecule DNA sequencing technology. One group has published a design for an instrument that could place a million single-molecule sequencers on a device the size of a postage stamp. To accomplish this, each sequencer will have an operating volume of one zeptoliter—much less than one billionth of one billionth of a liter! There can be no doubt that within a few years, most individuals will have their genome sequenced and encoded as part of their medical record. And this is just the beginning.

Nanotech Devices Capable of Detecting a Single Cancerous Cell

No equation can represent the astonishing technological trajectory we are on. The trek from Olduvai Gorge to Mesopotamia—from Homo habilis to the wheel—took 1.5 million years. A mere 5,500 years took us from the wheel to the double helix. Then 50 years to the human genome. Nanotechnology, our ability to build molecular devices with atomic precision, is the transcendent culmination of our co-evolution with tools. With the advent of nanomedicine, we will turn these tools inward.

The National Cancer Institute's fact sheet on nanotechnology and cancer says, "Most animal cells are 10,000 to 20,000 nanometers in diameter. This means that nanoscale devices (having at least one dimension less than 100 nanometers) can enter cells to interact with DNA and proteins. Tools developed through nanotechnology may be able to detect disease in a very small amount of cells or tissue. They may also be able to enter and monitor cells within a living body."

According to the National Institutes of Health [NIH], nanotechnology could create devices capable of reporting the onset of cancer at the exact moment of molecular metamorphosis, long before today's tests are effective. The key, as with DNA sequencing, is single-molecule sensitivity. One approach will use individual carbon nanotubes (molecular rods about half the diameter of the DNA molecule itself) to literally trace the physical shape of a single DNA molecule the way a phonograph needle traces a vinyl record. Another early-detection strategy will use … quantum dots (Q-dots). … Latex beads filled with these crystals will be designed to bind to specific DNA sequences. When the crystals are stimulated by a flash of light, they emit colors that light up the sequences of interest. By combining different-sized quantum dots in a single bead, scientists will create probes that release a spectral bar code specific for each type of cancer mutation.

Cancer-Killing Nanobots

Nanotechnology will also create tools to eradicate cancer cells without harming healthy cells. In therapy applications, as in detection, single-molecule recognition is the key. Each magic nanobullet will home in on a specific, targeted molecular structure. In fact, the goal is to treat cancer like an infectious disease. We will be vaccinated with nanoparticles that continuously circulate through the body. This cancer vaccine— really a primitive cancer-killing nanobot—will detect molecular changes, assist with imaging, release a therapeutic agent and then monitor the effectiveness of the intervention.

How close are we to cancer-killing nanobots? The NIH Web site talks about nanoshells—minuscule beads coated with gold. By manipulating the thickness of the layers constituting the nanoshells, scientists will design them to absorb specific wavelengths of light. The most useful nanoshells are those that absorb near-infrared light, which can easily penetrate into the body. Absorption of light by the nanoshells generates a lethal dose of heat. Researchers can already link nanoshells to antibodies that recognize cancer cells. In a "magic bullet" scenario, nanoshells will seek out their cancerous targets. Once they have docked, they will be zapped with near-infrared light. In laboratory cultures, the heat produced by light-absorbing nanoshells killed tumor cells while leaving neighboring cells intact. Experts believe quantum dots, nanopores and other devices may be available for clinical use in 5 to 15 years. Therapeutic agents are expected to be available within a similar time frame. Devices that integrate detection and therapy could arrive in the clinic in about 15 to 20 years, which means a cure for your Stage III melanoma and other forms of cancer could arrive within your lifetime.

Airbots, Bacterial Zappers, and Microbivores

Things like quantum-dot bar codes and magic bullets made of gold nanoshells are in the lab right now. But these therapies are not pure nanotechnology. Rather, they are a hybrid of nanotech, biotech and conventional chemotherapy. For true believers, the real revolution will come when scientists start building molecular devices from their component atoms. The wildest dreams of nanomedicine are displayed in the Nanomedicine Art Gallery [on the Web site of the Foresight Institute] where you can view illustrations and animations of futuristic phenomena including bronchial airbots, bacterium zappers, blood probes and microbivores. According to the artist, the microbivore is "a theoretical nanorobot" that will cruise our bodies in the relentless pursuit of bad actors. If we can program these bots to eat bacteria, we can program them to eat cancer cells: So microbivores will quickly morph into the sheriffs of the nano-West, clearing out evildoers and varmints of all stripes.

Not everyone believes that molecular assemblers will be viable. But with or without them, it's undeniable that revolutionary nanomedicine-based tools are on the way. And when they arrive, they'll turn our world upside down—and not always in a good way.

Tsunami of Nanomedical Choices

Nanomedicine will be one of the greatest boons in human history. It could eventually allow doctors to save millions of lives and prevent entire populations from contracting various diseases. But it could also push the cruel divide in medical access that already exists to the absolute limit. Those with access to nanomedicine will face a different cruel divide, created by the inevitable time lag between the availability of diagnostic tools and efficacious cures. This gap, perhaps a decade or more, will raise its own set of unprecedented ethical questions—ones that will get even thornier once those cures are available. In the near future this tsunami of nanomedical choices could literally drown our health care and insurance systems.

Some of these choices involve elective genetic selection. If we can find and reprogram cancer or diabetes genes, we can

A Medicine Man's Dream

Once nanomachines are available, the ultimate dream of every healer, medicine man, and physician throughout recorded history will, at last, become a reality. Programmable and controllable microscale robots comprised of nanoscale parts fabricated to nanometer precision will allow medical doctors to execute curative and reconstructive procedures in the human body at the cellular and molecular levels. Nanomedical physicians of the early 21st century will still make good use of the body's natural healing powers and homeostatic mechanisms, because, all else equal, those interventions are best that intervene least. But the ability to direct events in a controlled fashion at the cellular level is the key that will unlock the indefinite extension of human health and the expansion of human abilities.

Robert Freitas, "Welcome to the Nanomedicine Page,"
Foresight Institute, 1998–2006.

certainly find and reprogram genes for simple physical traits like height or eye color. Genetic engineering raised these questions, but nanomedicine ensures they are here to stay. The physiological genetics of more complex traits like personality, sexual orientation and antisocial behavior will not be far behind. Likewise, nanobots that circulate and release chemicals on cue need not be limited to medicinal applications. (Think of the fate of the liquor industry when ethanol-releasing bots are online.) The ethical and financial implications of these developments are obvious.

But long before we have cures, nanomedicine-based diagnostics will create its own vortex of urgent health care issues. In the less distant future, say 2012, single-molecule DNA sequencing will mean that your genome will become an integral part of your medical record along with all sorts of other biomolecular identifiers. Beyond DNA sequencing, the tools of nanobiotechnology will allow us to predict both the metabolic state and the ultimate fate of cells and tissues with increasing precision. As a result, medicine will enter a phase we might call "Cassandra and the bell curve"—an uneasy situation in which we can predict the future, but only partially, with the result that we never get a truly specific prophesy to believe in.

On a long enough timeline, this means a new arsenal of weapons for, among other things, the war on cancer. It will be the promised golden age of biopharmaceuticals. But meanwhile the smart money is in diagnostics.

Targeted Medicine and Sometimes Tragic Limbo

Lots of companies are eager to get in on the ground floor. In 2000, Celera Genomics made history as the private company that forced an international consortium of developed nations to share the glory of sequencing the human genome. Celera still markets the intellectual property created by this accomplishment, but the heavyweight champion of DNA sequencing is now vigorously pursuing a career in the ring of molecular diagnostics. Celera Diagnostics is focusing its discovery efforts on "identifying genetic variations associated with common, complex diseases." And it is "working to develop new diagnostic products and to improve human health through an approach we call Targeted Medicine."

In theory, targeted medicine (aka personalized medicine) sounds awesome, and whenever it's viable most of us will want it. But before it is perfected, it will leave all of us— patients, doctors, governments, health care providers and insurance companies—in a frustrating, confusing and sometimes tragic limbo. And even after it is viable, it will raise huge questions, ones for which there are no easy answers.

Consider recent progress in the molecular diagnostics of breast cancer. Breast cancer patients with the same stage of disease can have markedly different treatment responses. In practical terms this means that no woman with breast cancer, even from the same demographic, has exactly the same illness as any other. Each woman's cancer has its own unique genotype. Currently, conventional medical treatment with chemotherapy can reduce the risk of metastases by approximately one-third. However, clinical data also show that 70–80 percent of patients receiving chemotherapy do not, in fact, benefit from it. Put simply, at least seven out of every 10 women patients endure chemotherapy for nothing. The agonizing current dilemma for doctors and patients is that chemotherapy will prolong life for three of the 10 women, but we can't determine which three.

The plan is to use gene-scan data to predict which patients will benefit from chemo. In 2002, workers in the Netherlands used a DNA microarray to develop a gene expression profile that outperformed all currently used clinical parameters in predicting disease outcome. They suggested that their findings provided a strategy to select patients who would benefit from adjuvant therapy (i.e. chemotherapy and/or radiation). This information, originally published as basic research, reached the public in articles with encouraging titles like "New Study Could Cut Breast Cancer Overtreatment." In this article, a member of the research team was quoted as saying, "We have confirmed that we can predict with 90 percent certainty that a patient will remain free of breast cancer for at least five years." Since then things have improved, but only incrementally.

The key concept here is "a patient"—i.e. you or you but not her. This is the world of personalized medicine, made possible by gene-scan-powered molecular diagnostics. In a perfect future, these gene scans will tell us which seven women can decline chemotherapy. But in the immediate future, these scans will only tell us the probability that a woman can safely decline treatment. This probability will get better every year, but when will molecular diagnostics be reliable enough to base life-and-death decisions on?

"A Little Knowledge Is a Dangerous Thing. So Is a Lot."

This work on breast cancer is, literally, just the tip of the iceberg. Long before single-molecule DNA sequencing (or $1,000 genomes) hits the marketplace, thousands of labs around the world will be using standard biotechnology instrumentation such as DNA microarrays to create molecular profiles of people and populations. These profiles will be used to develop diagnostics for every major disease and disorder. Like reproductive cloning, this technology takes us to the very essence of what it means to be an individual. Unlike cloning, the field of molecular diagnostics is receiving almost universal acclaim as a worthy goal for the future of medicine.

"A little knowledge is a dangerous thing. So is a lot." Once again, Einstein provides the appropriate homily. Like the manifestation of Moore's law [which says that technology increases exponentially over time] in computing, improvements in molecular diagnostics and nanomedicine are astonishing but still leave us far short of where we need to be. Unlike for the next generation of semiconductor chips, the time to market for each new product in targeted medicine will be measured in human lives. Before we have the set of genetic profiles or the tools to treat all breast cancers, we will know enough to modify the treatment regimes of a few breast cancers, then enough to help some breast cancers, then enough to help many. At what point will this knowledge be allowed to enter the health care system? Will everyone have access to it? Who will pay for it? And who will make all these decisions?

Theoretical microbivores notwithstanding, no one seriously questions the transformative power of nanotechnology for human health. But it is equally true that no one understands how this revolution in personal medicine will impact a health care delivery system that, for many, is already hopelessly complex and frustrating.

Nanotech-Based Diagnostics and Personalized Medicine

New pharmaceuticals now reach the marketplace by showing efficacy in clinical trials based on the average response of a patient population. But nanotech-based diagnostics will open the option of personalized medicine, which, by definition, means that there is no longer an "average" response to therapy. Each patient's treatment regime should be unique. But there's no way we can do that with our existing health care system.

The reality is that we will have a world of molecular diagnostics long before we have a world of molecular cures. In the immediate future, gene scans will guide the use of conventional or biopharmaceutical therapies. In this world, women diagnosed with breast cancer will be advised that postoperative chemotherapy will not extend their survival. But this advice will come with a statistical caveat. More correctly, each patient will get her own prognosis with her own statistical caveat. The woman, her doctor, her insurance company and the government will all receive a statistically weighted prediction about her future. How are society, the government, private industry and the individual going to deal with this situation? The first act of the drama called personalized medicine will still be written by nature, the second by biotechnology, the third by nanotechnology. But who or what will be the author of the finale?

Within a generation, nanotechnology will completely invert our concept of medication. Today vaccines come with literature warning of a low probability that "some people" are subject to side effects or complications. In the age of nanotechnology-driven personalized medicine there will be no such thing as "some people." Theoretically, you should be able to know if you are that one in 10,000. But will you want to know? Will you be allowed to know? What will it cost to know, and who will pay? What if you could have known but didn't ask . . . or weren't told? And perhaps most disturbing of all: What if it turns out to be too expensive for society to pay for universal diagnosis, let alone treatment? Could we enter a world in which the rich live on and on, while the poor are denied even the knowledge of the disease that is inexorably killing them and whose prevention is at hand?

Our already faltering system was never designed for, nor can it handle, the flood of molecular diagnostic data that will reach biblical proportions within a decade. Just when we thought the web of health care delivery couldn't get any more tangled, patients, doctors and HMOs are about to meet the world of personal genome sequencing. Then will come gold nanoshells and, perhaps a bit later, microbivores.

And by the way, the proliferation of unique molecular identifiers will make medical privacy an impossibility because, ultimately, these types of data cannot be encrypted. The medium *is* the message. Millions of people have your fasting-blood-sugar value, but no one else on earth has your gene sequence. Get the idea? Any single-molecule-based nanomedical procedure could identify you beyond a shadow of a doubt. Yet a fundamental principle of nanomedicine is that billions of single-molecule fingerprints from DNA, RNA and proteins will be routinely available for diagnostic and therapeutic strategies. Which is the same as saying farewell forever to anonymity for your health records.

O brave new world, that has such genes in it!

"The most dangerous shortcomings from which a promising field like nanomedicine can suffer are a detachment from reality and overhyped expectations."

Nanomedicine Needs Realistic Goals

Kostas Kostarelos

In the following viewpoint, an editorial in the first edition of the journal Nanomedicine, *Kostas Kostarelos says that efforts in nanomedicine suffer when the field is overhyped. Kostarelos believes it is important to clearly define what is meant by nanomedicine, and he takes issue with some early, overly broad definitions of the term. According to Kostarelos, descriptions of miniscule nanobots floating through the bloodstream and zapping molecules of diseases more closely resemble science fiction than reality. Kostarelos believes these sorts of stories about nanomedicine do nothing to advance the field and in fact can harm its credibility. Kostarelos is the chair of Nanomedicine and deputy head at the*

Kostas Kostarelos, "The Emergence of Nanomedicine: A Field in the Making," *Nanomedicine*, vol. 1, June 2006, pp. 1–3. Copyright © 2006 Future Medicine Ltd. Reproduced by permission. www.futuremedicine.com.

Centre for Drug Delivery Research, University of London, School of Pharmacy. He is also the senior editor of the journal Nanomedicine.

As you read, consider the following questions:

1. What is the definition of nanomedicine that has been adopted in the journal *Nanomedicine*?

2. What examples does Kostarelos provide of novel nano-scale materials?

3. According to Kostarelos, nanomedicine should be encouraged to develop as a discipline based on what?

Most of us actively engaged in biomedical research came across the term 'nanomedicine' through the inspiring, yet overambitious, and at the time controversial writings of Robert Freitas and the Foresight Institute. In these early references to the term nanomedicine, the focus lay with the role and function of the elusive 'nanorobots' and the potential benefit they could bring to medical practice both in diagnosis and therapy. The word nanomedicine is considered less controversial and more acceptable to the worldwide scientific community today, however, an accurate definition and conceptual framework of the term is still a matter of hot debate.

Devising an Appropriate Definition

A fundamental problem associated with the term nanomedicine, ironically enough, stems from those early proponents of nanomedicine, who define the term as 'More than just an extension of "molecular medicine", nanomedicine will employ molecular machine systems to address medical problems, and will use molecular knowledge to maintain and improve human health at the molecular scale'. The problems with this definition are that:

Real Nanomedicines

Nanomaterial	Name & type	Pharmacological function	Disease
Nanomedicines in the clinic			
	Liposome 30–100 nm	Targeted drug delivery	Cancer
	Nanoparticle (iron oxide) 5–50 nm	Contrast agent for magnetic resonance imaging	Hepatic (liver)
Nanomedicines under development			
	Dendrimer 5–50 nm	Contrast agent for magnetic resonance imaging	Cardiovascular (Phase III clinical trial)
	Fullerene (carbon buckyball) 2–20 nm	Antioxidant	Neurodegenerative, cardiovascular (preclinical)
	Nanoshells (gold-coated silica) 60 nm	Hyperthermia	Cancer (preclinical)

TAKEN FROM: Kostas Kostarelos, "The Emergence of Nanomedicine: A Field in the Making," *Nanomedicine*, June 2006.

- By including 'molecular machine' and 'molecular knowledge' into the definition of 'nanomedicine' or 'medical nanotechnology' the whole of chemistry, physics and molecular biology are essentially included, in this way contradicting the novel and new nature of nanomedicine;

- It is much broader than the now defined and widely accepted term of nanotechnology, which includes 'materials that at least one of their dimension that affects their function is in the scale range between 1–100 nm' [nanometers];

- The close association of nanomedicine with non-realistic, futuristic and science-fiction-based imagery, such as nanorobots, can easily lead to negative perceptions about the term in the minds of the wider scientific and general public.

The result of the problematic definition and conceptual basis of nanomedicine leads to confusion and can also be responsible for undervaluing the credibility of this emerging field, which has been very recently highlighted in widely read science journals. We, in this journal [*Nanomedicine*], adopt the definition of nanomedicine as 'the use of materials, of which at least one of their dimensions that affects their function is in the scale range 1–100 nm, for a specific diagnostic or therapeutic purpose'. Our strong belief is that nanomedicine should be led by the clinical purpose it is designed to achieve. Our commitment is to attract the interest of the clinicians that eventually will be the end users of all the nanomedicine knowledge and technology generated. . . .

An Exciting Future

Irrespective of terms, definitions and linguistics, it is now accepted that nanomedicine is a field that is emerging and rapidly gaining acceptance and recognition as an independent field of research and technology. As our knowledge of physical properties at the nanoscale becomes more profound and novel nanometer-sized materials are developed, their use in biomedical applications will exponentially increase. Similar to the rest of nanotechnology, the novelty and significance of nanomedicine is in the new perspective and focus that it offers: the utilization of nanometer-scale materials to monitor, diagnose

Revolution Unlikely

One should therefore not expect nanomedicine to revolutionise medicine. It is one promising avenue by which medicine can advance. At the end of the day, it will have contributed new treatment-options for certain diseases, some new nanomedicines, better imaging-techniques and other diagnostic tools. These will add significantly to the currently available arsenal of therapies and medicines, raising similar ethical and societal concerns as did the medical advances of the past.

NanoBio-Raise, *"Nanomedicine,"* 2007.
http://files.nanobio-raise.org.

and cure diseases. It can be argued that all drug molecules can be considered nanomedicines since they act at the molecular level. Nanomedicine researchers should respond that their discipline is focusing at the nanoscale, which is above the molecular level and within the 100 nm scale. Whatever the argument, the fact is that nanometer-sized self-assembled systems and devices, such as drug delivery systems, have been developed for a number of years, having an established role in clinical practice today. This does not mean that nanomedicine has no further potential to improve clinical practice. On the contrary, consolidation of previously acquired knowledge on how nanoparticles act in the body with novel nanoscale materials (such as carbon nanostructures, quantum dots) and tools (e.g., sensors, high resolution imaging) give promise to a very exciting future for nanomedicine. . . .

Hype Hurts

What about the shortcomings of nanomedicine? These lie in the 'eye of the beholder'. The most dangerous shortcomings from which a promising field like nanomedicine can suffer are a detachment from reality and overhyped expectations. Nanomedicine should be encouraged to develop as a discipline based on scientifically proven realities rather than alluring science-fiction-based prospects and illustrations. Safety considerations, public awareness of what is feasibly possible and very close contact with reality and the needs of the clinician who will ultimately use the nanomedicine tools and knowledge will guarantee valuable contributions and benefits to patients. Nanomedicine and the construction of a comprehensive delivery system for surveillance, monitoring, treatment and elimination of disease may be an elusive goal to achieve, but provides great motivation for a creative process that can serve and benefit medical practice.

The image of a miniscule-sized vessel navigating through the blood stream, moving through organs, surveying the whole body for unwanted pathogens or malignancies and obliterating them on-demand by use of a laser or tweezers is a truly fascinating concept that has become a cinematographic reality on numerous occasions since the 1950s. The close relationship between scientific paradigm and science fiction illustrations has been tantalizing for both sides. What about reality though? Can nanotechnology assist with its tools and knowledge to achieve such a challenging goal for medicine? This is precisely the role of nanomedicine and all of us involved in this captivating, yet onerous, effort.

> *"Hype or excitement about nanomedi-*
> *cine should not obscure the important*
> *ethical and societal implications of*
> *these technologies."*

The Ethical Implications of Nanomedicine Must Be Considered

Raj Bawa and Summer Johnson

In the following viewpoint, Raj Bawa and Summer Johnson as-
sert that it is critical that the ethical, societal, and regulatory is-
sues of nanomedicine are discussed before the technologies are
clinically used. Bawa and Johnson discuss various questions
about nanomedicine that need resolution. These questions in-
clude: What is the morality of using nano-based procedures for
human enhancement? What are the long-term risks of nano-
medicines? And, how can government protect the privacy of
health information? According to Bawa and Johnson, these ques-
tions, and other concerns about nanomedicine, must be ad-
dressed to ensure fairness and safety so that nanomedicine can
provide the greatest benefits to society. Bawa is the president of
Bawa Biotech consulting and a professor in natural and applied

Raj Bawa and Summer Johnson, "The Ethical Dimensions of Nanomedicine," *The Medi-cal Clinics of North America*, vol. 91, 2007, pp. 881–887. Copyright © 2007 Elsevier, Inc. All rights reserved. Reproduced by permission. www.nvcc.edu.

sciences at Northern Virginia Community College. Johnson is the director of the Ethics in Novel Technologies, Research, and Innovation program of the Alden March Bioethics Institute.

As you read, consider the following questions:

1. What do the authors say is essential for greater public acceptance of nanomedicine and which is also critical for its commercial viability?

2. According to the authors, both enhancement and therapy are based on the relative concept of what?

3. According to the authors, why is there a concern that the retention of nanomedicine molecules in the body may cause long-term harm to healthy tissues?

Medical practice is about to enter a new era focused on the nanoscale and the practice of "nanomedicine." Nanomedicine may be defined as the monitoring, repair, construction, and control of human biological systems at the molecular level, using engineered nanodevices and nanostructures. Nanomedicine is, in a broad sense, the application of nanoscale technologies to the practice of medicine, namely, for diagnosis, prevention, and treatment of disease and to gain an increased understanding of complex underlying disease mechanisms. The creation of nanodevices, such as nanobots capable of performing real-time therapeutic functions in vivo [inside the human body], is one long-term goal. Advances in delivering nanotherapies, miniaturization of analytic tools, improved computational and memory capabilities, and developments in remote communications will eventually be integrated. These efforts will cross new frontiers in the understanding and practice of medicine. The ultimate goal is comprehensive monitoring, repair, and improvement of all human biologic systems—basically, an enhanced quality of life.

A Huge Impact

The potential impact of nanomedicine on society could be huge. Nanomedicine could drastically improve a patient's quality of life, reduce societal and economic costs associated with health care, offer early detection of pathologic conditions, reduce the severity of therapy, and result in improved clinical outcome for the patient. Numerous companies are actively involved in nanomedicine research and development, with many nanomedicine-related products already on the market or under development. The nanopharma market is expected to grow significantly in the coming years. Analysts project that by next year [2008] the market for nanobiotechnology will exceed $3 billion, reflecting an annual growth rate of 28%. According to another recent report, the United States demand for nanotechnology-related medical products (nanomedicines, nanodiagnostics, nanodevices, and nanotech-based medical supplies) will increase more than 17% per year to $53 billion in 2011 and $110 billion in 2016. This report predicts that the greatest short-term impact of nanomedicine will be in therapies and diagnostics for cancer and central nervous system disorders. Yet, despite all of this research and development in nanomedicine, federal funding related to the research and educational programs on ethical issues have clearly lagged behind. It is critical that ethical, social, and regulatory aspects of nanomedicine be proactively addressed to minimize public backlash similar to that seen with other promising technologies, most notably, genetically modified foods in Europe. The public should be properly educated regarding the benefits and risks of nanomedicine. Such an approach is essential for greater public acceptance and support for nanomedicine. In fact, it is critical for commercial viability of nanotechnology in general.

Given this backdrop, it is possible that nanomedicine is poised to add a profound and complex set of ethical questions for health care professionals. Once nanobased interventions are tested in clinical trials and given Food and Drug Administration (FDA) approval, it becomes the domain of health care practitioners to use nanotechnology for the improvement of human health and populations. But for many physicians, nanomedicine is an entirely new area for preventive and diagnostic interventions and curative therapies that will require continuing education, patient education, and a heightened awareness of the risks for and benefits of nanotechnologies as applied to medicine. We will focus primarily on issues that are likely to emerge once nanomedicine moves out of the preclinical and clinical stages of research and development. In other words, our discussions will be limited to nanomedicine products as they enter the market and find medical applications in diagnosis, prevention, and treatment of disease.

Nanomedicine raises fundamental questions, such as what it is to be human, how human disease is defined, and how treating disease is approached. Just as with the era of genetics and molecular biology, physicians will have to reconceptualize how they think about the diseases they treat, the means they have to treat them, and the meaning of the phrase, "do no harm."

Yet, nanomedicine is not a single class of medical interventions that can easily be analyzed from an ethical perspective. Nanomedicine includes a wide range of technologies that can be applied to medical devices, materials, procedures, and treatment modalities. The simplest way to distinguish categories of nanomedical interventions is to differentiate diagnostic nanomedicine from therapeutic nanomedicine. Diagnostic nanomedicine can include a wide range of interventions, from the use of nanoparticles for detecting tumors or cells with imaging technologies to chips or other implantable devices that can be created using nanoparticles and nanotechnology techniques that can be used to monitor or detect changes in blood chemistry, DNA, or other materials. It has been postulated that by 2016, clinicians or health care workers will be capable of scanning an entire genome within a few minutes. Therapeutic nanomedicine includes a wide range of interventions—from nanopharmacology to nanobased medical devices, such as surgical nanobots or drug-delivery devices to nanomaterials used for bone grafts or other body implants.

Just as different ethical issues exist for preventive medicine versus curative or therapeutic medicine, there exist very different kinds of ethical issues that arise out of diagnostic nanomedicine versus therapeutic nanomedicine. Interventions based on nanotechnologies likely will resurrect old questions about human enhancement, human dignity, and justice that have been asked many times before in the context of pharmaceutic research, stem cell research, and gene therapy.

Much of what is discussed or "hyped" as the future of nanomedicine, however, has yet to occur. Therefore, it is difficult for ethicists to predict in advance of the arrival of actual technologies what kinds of issues might arise out of nanomedicine. Yet, on the basis of other kinds of biomedical technologies that have affected health care, it is possible to conjecture what some of the perennial ethical issues and novel ethical problems for nanomedicine will be. Therefore, this article outlines a range of potential ethical issues for preventive and therapeutic nanomedicine that may occur as these technologies move from the laboratory to the clinic. Specific focus is on the ethical question of enhancement versus therapy, the risk for and benefits of nanotechnologies in health care, changing understanding of human disease, and privacy and confidentiality.

Understanding Human Disease

Diagnostic nanotechnologies eventually will provide the ability to detect and characterize individual cells, subtle molecular changes in DNA, or even minor changes in blood chemistry—scenarios that will likely cause pause and reconsideration of what it means to be a "healthy person" versus a "person who

Don't Let Ethics Lag Behind

Despite the enormous promise of nanomedicine, and the considerable funding going into the field, the research into the ethical, legal and social implications of nanomedicine is comparatively minute. As Peter Singer wrote in his 2003 tutorial "Mind the gap: science and ethics in nanotechnology": "The science leaps ahead, the ethics lags behind." As with nanotechnology in general, there is danger of derailing nanomedicine if the study of ethical, legal and social implications does not catch up with scientific developments.

Cathy Garber,
"The Potential and the Pitfalls of Nanomedicine,"
Nanowerk.com, May 7, 2007.

has a disease." In a "nanoworld," we might have to reconsider how to diagnose someone who has, say, cancer. Is the presence of a genetic mutation known to have a predisposition for causing cancer in a single cell a diagnosis? Or is it simply a risk factor? How many cells from the body must be of a cancerous nature for it to be defined as cancer? 1? 50? 1000? The answers to these questions are difficult because at this point no one knows exactly how to define, diagnose, or detect disease with this level of sensitivity. Eventually, disease may be able to be detected in this way, but it is important to remember that the development of such diagnostic technologies will require reconceptualizing understanding of disease. This will have a significant impact on health care professionals and patients.

The key is that if the slightest abnormality *can* be discovered, one must ask whether or not such information will have clinical relevance. If such knowledge does have clinical relevance, then it seems reasonable to develop technologies that could detect diseases at their earliest stages with the hope that this early detection would result in fewer side effects, less aggressive treatments, and better survival rates.

There may be some cases, however, where more information is simply too much information. Such heightened awareness simply could result in anxious patients, worried family members, or an entire group of the "worried well." One must, therefore, think carefully about which diseases and conditions it would be appropriate to apply such nanotechnologies to so that those interventions are helpful in understanding those diseases, rather than creating a burden or risk for patients and others. Therefore, the balance of information processed and disseminated versus benefit to society and individual health is a significant consideration for the ethics of nanotech-based diagnostic technologies.

Enhancement Versus Therapy

A related distinction for judging the morality of a medical procedure or treatment is whether or not it is regarded as therapeutic or enhancing—a subjective determination that is coupled with the determination of whether or not the procedure or treatment results in a normal or abnormal individual. A little analysis, however, reveals these distinctions to be unavailing because both enhancement and therapy are based on the relative concept of "normal". Most novel medical technologies that are employed for diagnosis, prevention, or treatment of diseases can also be used to enhance the function of the human body or mind. The traditional distinction between therapy and enhancement lies in the fact that therapy is concerned with maintaining, repairing, or restoring bodily parts or functions that a patient previously had or used. Enhancement, however, is concerned with the creation or improvement of bodily parts or functions that were absent, undamaged, or previously malfunctioning. Using this distinction, the implantation of a nanoscale device that emulates the function of a congenitally absent organ paradoxically would be enhancing rather than therapeutic.

As to this question, a frank prohibition pragmatically is unworkable. There are simply too many potential benefits that implantable nanoscale medical devices offer, and policing their use will only be effective when society has reliable methods to detect violations.

Rather, at the level of the profession, the practice of nanomedicine must be governed by a nanomedical ethic that maps the classical principles onto a transhuman and posthuman reality. Of these, the principle of "justice" in access to nanomedical procedures and entitlement to nanomedical treatment likely will be the most contentious. In this context, issues relating to unfair competition, socio-economic inequality, discrimination, and bias will arise and need to be addressed. At the level of civilization, a morality must be crafted that honors an unprecedented expansion in the meaning of human being and militates against any eugenics [advancement of the human race through selective breeding] agenda.

Risk Versus Benefit

Another important concern for nanomedicine is the need to balance the potentially significant benefits of nanomedical interventions with their potential risks. In the area of therapeutic nanomedicine, for example, it is clear that nanotechnologies will allow active chemical compounds or drugs to be more bioavailable and targeted to specific cellular structures. Therefore, these compounds will be needed at lower doses and have fewer side effects. One likely risk of nanomedicine, however, is that these drugs will receive FDA approval and be on the market long before the long-term risks are conclusive. Because nanomedicines have the potential to cross the blood-brain barrier or enter cells easily, it is a concern that the retention of these molecules in the body may cause long-term or unintentional harm to healthy tissues. Because long-term follow-up data regarding nanomedicines do not yet exist, it is important that patients be informed, that there may be long-term consequences for using these drugs. Although this is not altogether different from the long-term risks associated with exposure to chemotherapeutic or radiologic agents, it is an important risk factor that must be disclosed to patients taking nanomedicines or any kind of intervention involving nano-particles or nanomaterials.

Privacy and Confidentiality

Another important ethical issue relates to the protection and maintenance of health information in the era of nanomedicine. Nanotechnologies will make possible the collection of an enormous amount of individual cellular/subcellular level surveillance data of the human body. Nanomedical technology is expected to miniaturize implantable devices so that they function at the subcellular or synaptic level with the ability to monitor or collect data regarding cellular activities and biochemical events within organs, tissues, or individual cells. One application of this technology would be to include a means by which that information could be transmitted remotely. For example, the VeriChip Corporation has declared the availability of the world's first and only patented, FDA-cleared radiofrequency identification implantable microchip. The VeriChip is inserted under the skin and can be easily scanned with a reader. A small amount of radiofrequency energy passes from the reader energizing the dormant microchip, which then emits a radiofrequency signal transmitting an individual's unique verification number. This number then can be used for various purposes, including accessing personal medical information from a database or assessing whether or not somebody has authority to enter into a high-security area.

If and when such technologies are made possible via nanotechnology, a key ethical question arises: Can the health information infrastructure handle, collect, process, and analyze real-time on-going health data? With so few health care institutions adopting electronic medical record systems or health information systems designed to accommodate increasingly large medical files across institutions and time periods, it is of concern that ways are being created to generate massive amounts of health information without a system to use it. Moreover, ensuring privacy and confidentiality in such a system would be of utmost importance; a system without adequate safeguards presents serious ethical problems.

It is difficult to predict how ethical issues related to nanomedicine will evolve in the years to come. Nevertheless, ethical considerations will likely play a significant role in the development and use of nanotechnologic interventions in medical care. Initially, some of the important ethical concerns will continue to focus on risk assessment and environmental management. Later on, novel ethical issues and unforeseen dilemmas will arise as the field advances further and intercepts other areas of biomedical research, including genomics, personalized medicine, bioinformatics, and neurobiology. As with other biotechnologic advances before it, nanomedicine will face significant challenges as it moves from proof-of-concept to clinical trials to clinics. Along the way, ethical questions regarding social justice, privacy, confidentiality, long-term risks and benefits, and human enhancement are certain to arise. Health care providers must be ready to answer such ethical questions for themselves and be able to address those questions for their patients. Ultimately, it seems likely that nanomedicine will usher in a new area in health care where pharmaceuticals will be more effective and less toxic, where disease monitoring can be done on a highly sensitive and specific level, and where injections, surgical procedures, and a host of other interventions will be made, less painful, less toxic, and with fewer side effects than their current counterparts. It is important to ensure, however, that these advances in medical care do not come at the expense of fairness, safety, or basic understanding of what it means to be a healthy human being. Ultimately, public and political interest for regulations need to be carefully balanced with the interests of scientists and businesses for uninhibited science and technological efforts. Hype or excitement about nanomedicine should not obscure the important ethical and societal implications of these technologies. Nanomedicine's future appears brightest if it can be assured that it also will be a future where such ethical issues are addressed by the health care profession.

"I find nothing noble or proper in the retention of our imperfections, particularly when it comes to diseases and the ravages of aging."

Nanomedicine Will Reshape Humanity for the Better

George Dvorsky, as told to Laura Sheahen

The following viewpoint is an interview of George Dvorsky with Laura Sheahen of Beliefnet.com, a spirituality Web site. Dvorsky is a transhumanist—he supports using technology to overcome human limitations, whether physical or mental. Sheahen asks Dvorsky about his thoughts on the use of nanomedicine-based technologies to enhance human beings. Dvorsky says that nanotechnologies offer unprecedented opportunities for people suffering from medical conditions or injuries. Additionally, he views the use of nanotechnology to increase people's cognitive ability as a move toward social justice. Dvorsky believes that using technology to alleviate human suffering is a noble endeavor. Dvorsky is the president of the Toronto Transhumanist Association.

George Dvorsky, as told to Laura Sheahen, "Nanotechnology Will Reshape Humanity," Beliefnet.com, 2007. Reproduced by permission. www.beliefnet.com.

As you read, consider the following questions:

1. Is Dvorsky concerned about a surveillance society where humans are constantly tracked and monitored?

2. What is Dvorsky's remedy for concerns about cosmetic neurology being used to make us less than human?

3. What does Dvorsky think that enhancement technologies will give future artists and everyday people?

*W*hat advantages or benefits do you see coming from nanotechnology in the future?

Molecular nanotechnology is poised to reshape humanity and redefine the human condition. Nanotech win be used to clean the environment, ease the pressure for natural resources, treat diseases and supplement the human body. It may even usher in a post-scarcity economy and help people in developing countries tackle hunger, child mortality, environmental degradation and diseases such as malaria and HIV/AIDS.

Looking to more futuristic scenarios, molecular nanotechnology may help in the development of new materials (such as diamondoid surfaces), increase human life span to unprecedented levels, augment human capacities, and even assist in the "reanimation" of individuals currently frozen in cryonic stasis.

Nano Concerns

What problems, crimes, or disadvantages do you foresee?

The problems are quite severe—some of them may be untenable. There is the apocalyptic possibility, for example, for self-replicating "run-away" nanotechnology to destroy the Earth's ecosystem. This is the so-called grey goo scenario.

Other problems include the development of weapons based on nanotech, like microscopic devices that attack the human nervous system or that generate an entire armada from a single seed.

Molecular nanotechnology may bring unprecedented good, but it may also undermine our species.

How would you answer critics concerned about a surveillance society—constant monitoring and tracking?

I am one of these concerned critics. The growing fear of novel terrorist threats, like the deliberate engineering of a catastrophic pathogen, is pushing society in the direction of ubiquitous [seemingly everywhere] surveillance. Also, there are commercial interests in these monitoring technologies; companies are eager to track their customers and the products they purchase. This is a legitimate privacy concern.

There are two ways in which citizens can protect themselves. The first is to strengthen those democratic processes that guarantee civil liberties, due process and institutional accountability. The second prescription is what author David Brin refers to as the "transparent society." We may have no choice but to tolerate an utter lack of privacy, but it will be crucial that we retain our ability to watch the watchers and hold them accountable for their actions.

How can society minimize crimes committed via nanotechnology?

A stronger United Nations and a monitoring/licensing agency with global support and reach would be a good start. Corporations will need to be monitored to ensure that their manufacturing processes and applications are not in violation of environmental and privacy laws. At the same time, legislators will have the daunting task of having to keep up to speed on the development and application of nanotechnology so that they can anticipate and prevent potential abuse.

What About Human Enhancement?

Will people be able to "upgrade" their brains by using chips and similar things?

"Chips," or what is more commonly referred to as cybernetics, is certainly one possibility. Other biotechnologies that

Extreme Makeover: Brain Edition

In the future, reality shows may have names such as *Extreme Makeover: Brain Edition* or *Sharp Eye for the Dumb Guy*.

At the beginning of each episode, viewers could learn about one hapless soul's lifelong struggles with algebra and another's desire to stop being a worrywart. By the end of the hour, the transformed contestants would be winning chess matches and prancing carefree through fields of daisies. Don't check the TV listings yet, but the idea is not all fantasy.

Some neurologists recently have wondered whether their field is the next frontier in elective medicine. The specialty now tries to protect ailing brains from conditions such as Parkinson's disease or migraine headaches. But doctors' efforts one day may extend to normal brains. . . .

There's even a name for the field: cosmetic neurology.

Laura Beil,
"Brain-Boosting 'Cosmetic-Neurology' on the Horizon,"
Dallas Morning News/Seattle Times, *November 6, 2004.*

will result in increased intelligence, better memory and improved emotional control include genomics, nanotechnology and neuropharmaceuticals.

There are people alive today who are already reaping the benefits of these technologies. Paraplegics are using neural interface devices to control computers, allowing them to type, move pointers, and play games with their minds. Synthetic neurons have been created that have taken over the processing responsibilities of dead or dying neurons (conditions that are brought about by such diseases as Alzheimer's); humans will soon be using cybernetic prostheses [artificial devices] to assist in cognition.

Cognitive modifications are also a way to alleviate the arbitrariness of the genetic lottery. A strong ethical case can be made that the availability of such enhancements will help us work toward social justice.

There are concerns that "cosmetic neurology"[1] and related things will make us less than human.

This is a concern that has a very simple remedy: common sense. People will collectively stop hammering nails into their hands once they realize it hurts. Aside from the vagueness of what it means to be human, or what constitutes a person who is "more" or "less" than human, the idea behind these technologies is to reduce suffering and to foster meaningful lives.

Neurotechnologies, whether they are cybernetic or pharmaceutical, will offer unprecedented opportunities for individuals to overcome psychological disorders and to improve the quality of their emotional lives. The Dalai Lama once said, "My Tibetan goals are the same as those of Western science: to serve humanity and to make better human beings."

How do you react to fears that nano-enhanced humans will become supercomputing brains with powerful machine-enhanced bodies, lording it over the plebes who can't afford chips?

The rich and powerful are already lording over the lower classes, particularly those in the developing world. The suggestion that enhancement technologies will suddenly invent this situation is a disturbing fiction.

As science fiction author Bruce Sterling once said, "The future is here, it's just not evenly distributed yet." The goal for future societies will be to make these new technologies as widely accessible and affordable as possible. We need to better promote the idea of universal health care. While initial costs

---

1. Cosmetic neurology is the name of a new field of medicine where medicine or pharmaceuticals are used to enhance cognitive abilities.

will be prohibitive for most, like any technology the costs will quickly drop and eventually be made available to the wider population.

Will art really be art if the artist's brain is enhanced by technology? For example, a painter or musician?

Art will be art so long as there are artists who claim that they are making art.

Art and technology are indelibly linked; all artists employ technique in their work and/or use tools to assist with their creations or performances.

Cognitively gifted individuals have created some of our most cherished works of art. Leonardo DaVinci may have been the most brilliant person who has ever lived (among his many talents, he could write two different sentences simultaneously with both hands). Most of the great composers, including Mozart and Beethoven, had perfect pitch and other cognitive endowments.

Enhancement technologies will not only give future artists unprecedented skills, they will also allow everyday people like you and me to engage as deeply into art as any of history's greatest artists. Augmentation technologies will democratize and better distribute talent.

Suffering Doesn't Make Us More Human

Some people feel that certain types of suffering or "malfunctioning," while unpleasant, can make us more human and more empathetic: for example, living with mild memory loss. Will we be less human if everything about us—our minds, our memories, our bodies—is "fixed"?

The notion that suffering is what makes us empathetic is an overly simplistic and outdated notion. Very young children and sociopaths lack this capacity, and no amount of suffering will add to their ability to empathize.

I find nothing noble or proper in the retention of our imperfections, particularly when it comes to diseases and the ravages of aging. Ethicists should be concerned about those actions that arc humane and good rather than those actions that infringe on some abstract and inviolable notion of what it means to be human.

> "What they want to do is use machines
> to turn us into cyborgs, half—human,
> half-machine things."

Nanomedicine Can Hurt Humanity

Nigel Cameron, as told to Laura Sheahen

In the following viewpoint, Laura Sheahen of Beliefnet.com, a spirituality Web site, interviews Nigel Cameron, president of the Institute on Biotechnology and the Human Future, and director of the Center on Nanotechnology and Society. Laura Sheahen asks Cameron why he believes it is inhuman to use nanotechnology for human enhancement. Cameron responds that people who would use machines and other nanotechnologies to increase their cognitive ability could become so smart they will cease to be human. Cameron thinks these people would have so much power they would rule the rest of the world. Cameron thinks that it is okay to use nanomedicine to help the mentally handicapped or for use in the arts. Cameron believes these kinds of uses help people to become more human, rather than less.

As you read, consider the following questions:

1. Does Cameron think that cancer will be cured with nano-delivery devices by 2015?

2. Does Cameron think that people become cyborgs when they have their hip replaced?

3. Where was Cameron when he said "the case has not been made that putting chips in your brain so you can remember your logorhythmic tables, or putting Google behind your right eye, is an enhancement?"

Laura Sheahen, Beliefnet: Can you explain what nanotechnology is?

Nigel Cameron: Nanotechnology is a term used for miniaturization in all areas of science. A nanometer is a billionth of a meter, and science—chemistry, engineering—is now pressing down to this level of manipulation. The future is there: it's where we'll have the most power to manipulate the natural order, and that's why it's so exciting, but it's also why it raises such big questions.

We will be able to miniaturize everything. For example, those tags you have on groceries in the store, which are radio frequency identifiers, are going to get smaller and almost free—so small you can't see them. This is great for inventory control in Wal-Mart—every product you ever buy could be tracked forever. But issues of privacy and confidentiality are raised in profound ways.

Is It Okay to Track People?

Could someone put the small thing that's normally on a CD in Wal-Mart into my sandwich? If I eat it, can I be tracked?

Indeed so, unless you have a mechanism that requires these things to be deactivated at point of sale or in some other way. And of course you could still get criminals using them.

Most of the sunscreen now sold in the U.S. contains nano-sized particles. I have no reason to believe they are not safe, but there are huge debates about how we deal with particles that are so small they can cross the blood-brain barrier. We have very little evidence of their long-term impact and the whole toxicology issue is enormously complicated.

In terms of tracking people, what problematic scenarios can you envision?

Well, you don't have to be a sci-fi writer or conspiracy theorist to see this as the end of privacy. If you have a government or commercial industries who want to know where everybody is, a surveillance society becomes much more practicable. Already you can put chips in your dog to find it if it strays.

At the other end of the scale, there's talk about using a nano-device to create clean water.

You'd be able to drop some little particles in dirty water, and . . .?

—and it would just clean it all up, little machines that would replicate and eat up all the impurities. It sounds wonderful. On the other hand, you say what is the context for this? Maybe someone comes along and patents it and says, "You can't use this unless you pay."

This all feeds into the need for a policy discussion based on a notion of human values.

What health applications of nanotechnology can you envision?

Well, the National Cancer Institute on its Web site says that by 2015, cancer will be cured or be controllable as a chronic condition using nano-delivery devices as a way of getting drugs into cells.

I think it's a somewhat irresponsible claim, because I'm sure it won't happen by 2015. But some of the hopes for these

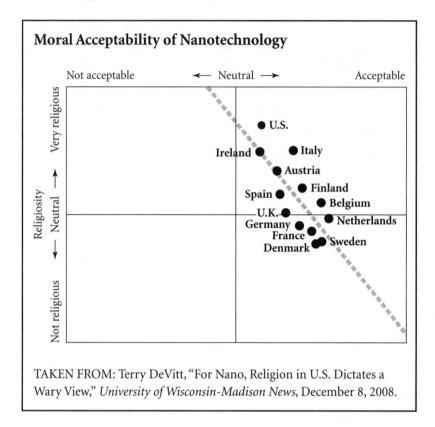

Moral Acceptability of Nanotechnology

TAKEN FROM: Terry DeVitt, "For Nano, Religion in U.S. Dictates a Wary View," *University of Wisconsin-Madison News*, December 8, 2008.

technologies are incredible, and we have to enthuse and support the *technology*, even while, at the same time, having a conversation about its responsible use.

Transhumanists Want to Turn People into Cyborgs

Some people think we should permanently incorporate tiny machines into our bodies to fix things.

There are people called transhumanists. Some of them are very engaging people, sort of sci-fi cultists, but now becoming part of the mainstream discussion. They're scaring both people who like being human and people in the business community. What they want to do is use machines to turn us into cyborgs, half-human, half-machine things.

My impression was that if you were 80 years old and your arm joint had worn out, a machine would be put in to help with that, but you'd still have a human brain.

I have no problem with that. I have a sore knee right now! You don't become a cyborg by having a hip replaced. What the transhumanists want to do is use nano-devices to live a life that ceases to be human.

In what way would the transhumanist scenario be non-human?

For example, they want to take people who have not had a bang on the head and put chips in their brains, what they call neuroprostheses. You can wire up your neurons with a computer.

What if someone says "Gee, my human brain is great, but just like Keanu Reeves in The Matrix, *I'd like to learn judo"?*

Exactly. You can get the chip.

What Does It Mean to Be Human?

How is that not human?

When you ask yourself, what are the things that make humans most human? When are we being truest to ourselves? With these enhancements, like learning a new skill or getting rid of unpleasant memories—so-called cosmetic neurology—a term being used now in neurology journals for elective playing around with your brain ... you want to get over a traumatic experience, that's the kind of thing people are working on.

It's one thing to learn judo with a chip. What if you're wealthy and you want your 16-year-old to ace her SATs and you buy the upgrades and the chips?

You end up with the end of the human community, the new feudalism. You'll have some beings who cease to be human and become massively powerful computational machines, who are able to control global economy and politics. The rest become the serfs.

There's a naïve geekiness about those who talk about enhancing human nature without asking what human nature is.

At a Sandia conference about cognitive enhancement, I said the case has not been made that putting chips in your brain so you can remember your logorhythmic tables, or putting Google behind your right eye, is an enhancement. It may in fact be a degradation of what it means to be human. It's like giving a man one arm that's six feet long. Is that an enhancement? It would help him get stuff down from shelves in a store, but it would mess up his capacity to be human.

Let's not have this machine reductionism which is allied with technoutopianism [creating ideal societies through technology]. People like [transhumanist leader] Jay Hughes would call me a bioluddite [resistant to technology] or a "human racist."

If people see nano as a transhumanist thing, anything nano will be suspect in the market. There's real damage likely to be done to the good, healthy economic prospects of the *technology* by the prominence of the transhumanist ideas.

I say apply these to the arts, to our capacity to work with those who are mentally handicapped. Let's talk about what it means to be human, and then talk about how we can help us be more human.

Periodical Bibliography

The following articles have been selected to supplement the diverse views presented in this chapter.

Peter Cleaveland — "Nanotechnology: Huge Future for Small Innovation," *Medical Design Technology*, July 2007.

The Economist — "Swallow the Surgeon," September 4, 2008. www.economist.com.

Robert Freitas — "Nanotechnology and Radically Extended Life Span," *Life Extension Magazine*, January 2009. www.lef.org.

Sarah Fister Gale — "A Slow Road to Big Impact: Small Tech in Medicine," Smalltimes.com, March 2008. www.smalltimes.com.

James R. Heath, Mark E. Davis, and Leroy Hood — "Nanomedicine Targets Cancer," *Scientific American*, February 2009.

Sylvain Martel — "Enabling New Medical Interventions Through Medical Nanorobotics," SCITIZEN.com, June 26, 2007. www.scitizen.com.

Benjamin Melki — "Adriano Cavalcanti: Medical Nanorobotics for Diabetes," *NanoVIP*, January 31, 2007. www.nanovip.com.

Prachi Patel-Predd — "New Nano Weapon Against Cancer," *Technology Review*, July 2, 2007. www.technologyreview.com.

Katherine Phan — "Americans Reject Morality of Nanotechnology on Religious Grounds," *Christian Post*, February 18, 2008. www.christianpost.com.

ScienceDaily.com — "Nano-sized 'Cargo Ships' to Target and Destroy Tumors Developed," September 12, 2008. www.sciencedaily.com.

OPPOSING
VIEWPOINTS®
SERIES

C HAPTER 4

What Role Should the U.S. Play in Promoting or Regulating Nanotechnology?

Chapter Preface

Back in the 1990s, genetic engineering, or biotechnology, was hailed as a revolutionary new scientific technique that was going to transform medicine, bring food to the poor, and produce innovative new products. Biotechnology has provided many important scientific achievements, such as mass produced human insulin and the discovery of the breast cancer gene, BRCA1. Biotech products, however, have yet to achieve their touted destiny. Many people in the public are distrustful of biotechnology, particularly its use in foods. Many scientists and policy makers believe that in order for nanotechnology products to be successful, the nanotechnology industry must avoid the mistakes made by the biotech industry, and gain the public's trust.

The first biotech food product produced by the use of genetic engineering was a failure. In the 1990s, a company called Calgene introduced Flavr Savr tomatoes. The tomatoes were genetically modified to slow the softening process after picking. Safety concerns and other problems caused the tomatoes to be pulled from store shelves only a year or so after they were introduced. The tomatoes also cost more than regular tomatoes, didn't taste any better, and were prone to bruising.

The public became mistrustful of biotech products. Despite the failure of the Flavr Savr tomato, other genetically modified (GM) foods started appearing on store shelves. Unfortunately, the foods weren't labeled as GM. Consumers typically only became aware of them through sensationalized media reporting of industry missteps, such as when unapproved GM corn ended up in taco shells and corn flakes. Many environmental groups, particularly in Europe, vociferously opposed GM foods, calling them "frankenfoods." The bad publicity and the opposition of environmental groups caused the public to become leery of biotech foods.

Many scientists believe that the nanotechnology industry must court public opinion in order to avoid repeating the biotech industry's mistakes. According to Professor Lynn Frewer of the University of Wageningen in the Netherlands, "Consumers suspected companies of developing GM food for their own economic benefit and were not looking after consumer protection, and often the GM food was unlabelled, which meant people did not have a choice. The legacy of GM means that nanotechnology has a battle to win over public perception."

Studies have found that current public opinion on nanotechnology varies based on a person's values. A 2008 study conducted by the Cultural Cognition Project at Yale Law School in collaboration with the Project on Emerging Nanotechnologies (PEN) found that a person's cultural values largely determine their view of nanotechnology. When given certain information about nanotechnology, people who tend to be individualistic and pro-commerce are apt to decide that nanotechnology is safe. Alternatively, people who tend to worry about economic inequality, when given the same information, conclude that nanotechnology is dangerous. According to David Rejeski, the director of PEN, the message matters. "How information about nanotechnology is presented to the vast majority of the public who still know little about it can either make or break this technology," he says.

Nanotechnology organizations seemed to have gotten the message that public perception is important. One of the primary objectives of the U.S. National Nanotechnology Initiative (NNI) is to promote the public's acceptance of nanotechnology. According to the NNI, "Support for the continued advancement of nanotechnology research, and eventual integration of nanotechnology into consumer products and useful applications, will depend heavily on the public's acceptance of nanotechnology. Governments around the world must take a proactive stance to ensure that environmental, health, and safety concerns are addressed as nanotechnology research and development moves forward in order to assure the public that nanotechnology products will be safe."

The introduction of GM foods revealed that the industry must consider the public's attitudes toward an emerging technology. Nanotechnology proponents appear to be taking note. Government actions towards new technologies, such as promotion or regulation, can play an important part in the message the public receives about a new technology. In the following chapter, the authors consider what role the government should have in promoting or regulating nanotechnology.

> "More must be done—in both the amount of funding and the way that nanotech research is financed—for U.S. nanotech-based industries to stay apace with the rest of the world."

The U.S. Government Should Fund Nanotechnology Research

Jacob Heller and Christine Peterson

In the following viewpoint, Jacob Heller and Christine Peterson argue that the U.S. government should increase funding for nanotechnology research. The National Nanotechnology Initiative (NNI) is a program established by the U.S. government to promote and coordinate federal nanotechnology research. Heller and Peterson assert that the NNI's budget has been shrinking in recent years and the United States is beginning to fall behind other countries in the amount of government money provided to fund nanotechnology research. The authors believe federal funding is imperative for some types of beneficial, but financially risky, nanotechnology research. Private companies are hesitant to fund projects when the return on their investment is in doubt. If the United States wants to keep its lead in nanotechnology research, the government should provide more money, assert Heller and Peterson. Peterson is the president of the Foresight Nanotechnology Institute and Heller is a policy associate at the institute.

As you read, consider the following questions:

1. Heller and Peterson say that the NNI has made valuable contributions to nanotechnology development and they name four applications that NNI-funded researchers have been working on. What are these four applications?

2. How much does China spend each year on nanotech research, according to Heller and Peterson?

3. According to Heller and Peterson, the federal government should consider following Japan's example and do what?

The United States federal government leads the world in nanotechnology research and development funding. The National Nanotechnology Initiative (NNI), the federal government's R&D [research and development] program that coordinates multiagency efforts in nanotech science, allocates over $1 billion annually to 14 agencies. Since its inception in 2000 it has been largely regarded a success. Most recently, the President's Council of Advisors on Science and Technology (PCAST) found that the funding is "very well spent", and that "the program is well managed". However, some fear that the United States is beginning to lose its lead in nanotechnology research funding, and that the current structure of federal R&D is not optimally designed to promote the most innovative output. To maintain international leadership in the field of nanotechnology and promote the discovery of beneficial nanotechnology, the NNI will probably require more funding and a reevaluation of its structure.

Government Funding Has Been Fruitful

The NNI has already made valuable contributions to the development of nanotechnology. With NNI funding, researchers have been working on gold nanoshells that can target the destruction of malignant cancer cells, low-cost hybrid solar cells, quantum dots that can open the door to much faster computing, and nanoscale iron particles that can reduce the costs of cleaning up contaminated groundwater. Due largely to this high level of funding, the United States leads the world in nanotech patents, startups, and papers published.

However, more can and should be done. The United States is beginning to lose its lead in government-sponsored nanotech R&D relative to the rest of the world. When adjusted for purchasing-power-parity (a comparison of how much a dollar can buy in different countries), non-U.S. governments are spending more per-capita on nanotech research and development than the United States. Using this scale, the United States spent $5.42 per capita in government funding for nanotech R&D in 2004, while South Korea spent $5.62, Japan, $6.30, and Taiwan, $9.40. Other countries are quickly catching up. China spends $611 million annually (after adjusting for purchasing-power-parity) on nanotech research, nearly 40 percent of U.S. federal funding.

Instead of expanding government spending on nanotech to meet the challenge, funding increases for the NNI have not even kept pace with inflation. The proposed budget for FY [fiscal year] 2006 was actually lower than FY 2005 funding when adjusted for inflation . . .

Private Sector Unwilling to Fund Risky Research

It has been argued that the private sector, not government, should fund all nanotechnology research and development. However, even many libertarians—the group most skeptical of government involvement—take the position that private firms

Top Ten Countries in Public Nanotechnology R&D, 2006

**in millions of U.S. dollars
using currency exchange rates**

United States	1,775
Japan	975
Germany	563
France	473
South Korea	464
United Kingdom	280
China	220
Taiwan	132
Russia	106
Canada	61

TAKEN FROM: John F. Sargent, "Nanotechnology and U.S. Competitiveness: Issues and Options," *CRS Report for Congress,* May 15, 2008. Data from *Profiting from International Nanotechnology,* Lux Research, December 2006.

are unlikely to engage in long-term basic research when those firms will be unable to reap the full benefits of their investment. This type of basic research may constitute a public goods problem, in which market processes working alone may not function optimally. Foundation funding can make a difference, but is generally focused on specific applications such as the nanoemulsion-based vaccine delivery system recently funded by the Gates Foundation.

Sustained expansion in federal R&D funding may be critical to the development of U.S. nanotech-based industries. The federal government can fund long-term and risky research that companies are unwilling and unable to conduct; these types of research usually have the largest payoff for society in the long run. Also, at current budget levels, the federal government cannot fund many meritorious research efforts. The ratio of serious proposals to funded projects is too high; for example, in 2004 the NSF [National Science Foundation] received 48 proposals for funding nanotech research centers, but could only afford to finance six. Even when researchers do receive federal funding, the amounts are usually inadequate to completely and fully research a subject.

Government Should Modify Grant-Giving Process

Besides the amount of funding, the structure and duration of most NNI funded research is problematic. Because NNI budget pressures have made the peer review process more conservative and because most grants are given for only one year, many researchers essentially do the experiment before writing the grant to ensure year-after-year funding. This necessarily constrains risk-taking and creativity, both of which are essential for large-breakthroughs in nanotech research. The federal government should consider following Japan's example and fund research projects for durations as long as five years, or even more.

A triennial review of the National Nanotechnology Initiative issued by the National Research Council in 2006 also advocated changes to the research areas being covered. In addition to more focus on environmental, health, and safety concerns, the NRC looked specifically at the field of molecular manufacturing (molecular machine systems), recommending improved coordination between experimental and theoretical work in this highly promising area of nanotechnology.

There are also other ways to encourage nanotech research and innovation besides directly funding R&D efforts that the federal government should consider. For example, the federal government could offer prizes for specific innovations, or make commitments to purchase nanotechnological products if they are produced.

More must be done—in both the amount of funding and the way that nanotech research is financed—for U.S. nanotech-based industries to stay apace with the rest of the world and quickly grow to maturity.

> *"Nanotechnology may prove to be a re-
> markable technology that changes the
> way we live our lives. But that is not a
> certainty, and therein lies the first prob-
> lem with the explosive growth in fed-
> eral funding of nanotech."*

The U.S. Government Should Not Fund Nanotechnology Research

Declan McCullagh

*In the following viewpoint, Declan McCullagh contends that the
U.S. government should not provide large sums of money for
nanotechnology research. McCullagh says that governments are
not the best predictors of worthwhile research. In the past governments have thrown money at several failed endeavors. Additionally, government money always comes with strings attached,
says McCullagh. He believes that the private sector can, and will,
continue to fund nanotechnology research. According to McCullagh, there is no justification for huge amounts of government
funding flowing to nanotechnology research. McCullagh is a
journalist, computer programmer, and photographer.*

As you read, consider the following questions:

1. What are three examples of government-funded research programs that have led to benefits, according to McCullagh?

2. According to McCullagh, what is "rent seeking?"

3. According to McCullagh, in 2003, Philip J. Bond predicted that the global market for nanoproducts would reach how much by 2015?

Federal funding for nanotechnology, the science of manipulating matter at the atomic and molecular level, is increasing dramatically. At a time when budgets other than homeland security are shrinking or remaining constant, nanotech spending is set to double over a three-year period. In 2001, the National Nanotechnology Initiative received $422 million, and President [George W.] Bush is asking for $847 million for the 2004 fiscal year. About a third of that money would go to the National Science Foundation, a third to the Defense Department, and the remainder to the Department of Energy and other agencies. The U.S. government is spending big money on small technology.

Nanotechnology Hopes to Revolutionize Manufacturing

The term nanotechnology refers to working with materials in the 1- to 100-nanometer range, a process that could create useful new substances, aid in medicine, and accelerate computers. A nanometer is a billionth of a meter, which is about a hundred-thousandth of the diameter of a human hair, or a mere 10 times the diameter of a hydrogen atom. Nanotechnology's proponents hope to revolutionize the way manufacturing works. Instead of grinding, milling, and sawing materials in inefficient, top-down processes, materials would be manipulated at the molecular level instead.

Zyvex, a nanotech startup, describes the concept this way: "If we rearrange the atoms in coal we can make diamond. If we rearrange the atoms in sand—and add a few other trace elements—we can make computer chips. If we rearrange the atoms in dirt, water and air we can make potatoes." Silicon Valley is experimenting with silicon nanowires and carbon nanotubes, two structures that could eventually replace standard transistors on chips. First-generation nano-products already on the market include the stain-resistant fabric used in Lee Performance Khakis and Advanced Powder Technologies' ZinClear, a transparent sunscreen that offers better UV protection than zinc oxide.

Governments Are Not Good at Guessing

Nanotechnology may prove to be a remarkable technology that changes the way we live our lives. But that is not a certainty, and therein lies the first problem with the explosive growth in federal funding of nanotech. Governments' track record in guessing what technologies will be worthwhile is hardly perfect.

Take the telling example of Japan's Ministry of International Trade and Industry [MITI]. MITI's research and development efforts over the last two decades are marked by bets on the wrong technology and sponsorship of projects with unrealistic expectations. Its highly-touted Fifth Generation Computer project was intended to leapfrog the rest of the world in high-speed computing and artificial intelligence through adopting the PROLOG programming language. Then Japan's computer makers balked at the prospect of participating in what they viewed as a project merely of academic interest. The Fifth Generation program eventually died without meeting MITI's stated goals.

The United States veered in a similar direction in the 1980s with Sematech, the government-created chip making consortium. Sematech was born of fears that Japanese manufacturers would crush their American rivals, a prediction that—given the state of that country's economy today—seems terribly alarmist. Over an eight-year period, taxpayers gave about $800 million to 14 electronic companies that made about $800 million in combined profits every *month*. . . .

Some government-funded research has led to benefits. The Internet began life as a Department of Defense project. The space program has given us Teflon and Tang. The National Institutes of Health has helped us understand disease.

Private Funding Can Be Relied Upon

The best case for a government subsidy of R&D [research and development] is to fund vital research that the private sector would fail to do on its own. Proponents of government nanotech funding argue that, as in other "basic research" areas, corporations have only short-term profit horizons. They say that government must pay for basic research because that's not profitable—only applied research is.

This point has some validity, but there are two counter-arguments. First, private sources will pay for basic research. It may not be at the level that all researchers would prefer, but if it can lead to applied research results, the private sector will still do some of it. Second, nanotechnology includes a mix of early-stage research and late-stage research. Intel's latest generation of microprocessors likely qualifies as nanotechnology, but should Uncle Sam pay for the development of a hypothetical Pentium VI? Third, by having private funders, you avoid the public choice problems.

Problems with Mixing Science and Politics

Real-world subsidies rarely, if ever, follow the ideal found in economics textbooks. Instead, government-funded R&D in the real world is subject to the lobbying and rent-seeking that takes place whenever government dangles money. As the nascent world of nanotechnology develops, we have a chance to

Where Has the Money Gone?

By the end of 2005 governments had sunk eighteen billion dollars of taxpayers money into nanotechnology R&D. With an additional six billion dollars forecast for 2006, nanotechnologies will then have received the same level of funding in absolute dollar terms as the entire Apollo program.

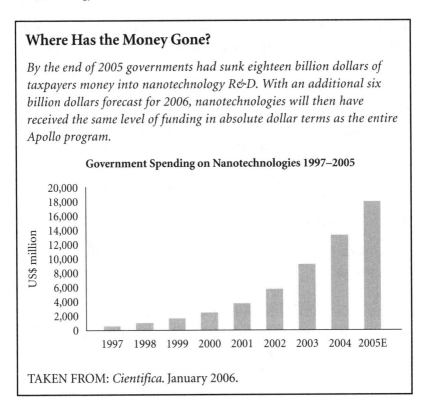

Government Spending on Nanotechnologies 1997–2005

TAKEN FROM: *Cientifica*. January 2006.

see how the political process steers research in political ways that need not parallel scientific goals.

Bureaucrats, special interest groups, and members of Congress have strong incentives to channel nanotech funds to politically popular recipients or into trendy research areas that may or may not have legitimate scientific value. This has already lent itself to pork-barrel politics, as illustrated by a March 2002 speech by House Science Committee Chairman Sherwood Boehlert (R-NY) delivered in New York City. In it, Boehlert pledged to steer a disproportionate amount of cash to businesses and universities in his home state. "I will do everything in my power to ensure that nanotechnology research gets the funding it deserves," Boehlert said. "I will do everything possible to see that a significant portion of that research takes place right here in New York state."

Without the traditional yardstick of profit and loss, there is no straightforward way to measure what is a wise course of spending. Rational economic calculations tend to be replaced by the routine of a guaranteed budget increase every year. Money often goes to favored or well-connected groups, and controversial but promising research may be ignored. Replacing market decisions with ones made on Capitol Hill could lead to highly-politicized results and inefficient allocation of nanotech funds.

Consider the debate over global warming. Richard Lindzen, the Alfred P. Sloan professor of meteorology at MIT [Massachusetts Institute of Technology], warned Congress in 1996 that researchers who relied on hefty government grants had strong incentives to exaggerate the potential problem. "A major source of support was seen as depending on the perpetuation of an issue rather than on a focused attempt to solve basic questions in a prioritized manner," Lindzen said. "Politicization contributed to this by establishing that agreement as to the possibility of crisis constituted public virtue, while scientific questioning was frowned upon to put it mildly." Myron Ebell, who specializes in science policy at the Competitive Enterprise Institute in Washington, says it's a problem plaguing government-funded R&D in general. "The only way to get the attention of the federal government is to create a big problem," Ebell told me. "As soon as the scientific community learned the answers, there's zero money. If there isn't a problem, they don't get the money."

Tying Strings to Funding

Government funding of nanotech-research also tends to lead to increased government control. That has happened in other areas, for example when Congress linked highway funding to drinking ages and required schools and libraries receiving federal funds to install Internet filtering software. In August 2001,

President Bush signed a controversial executive order limiting federal funding for cloning research to about 60 existing stem cell lines.

It's too early to predict what might happen in the case of nanotechnology, but early signals indicate Congress is eager to tie strings to funding. A bill introduced by Sen. Ron Wyden (D-OR) would "ensure that philosophical, ethical, and other societal concerns will be considered alongside the development of nanotechnology." [The legislation was not enacted.] During a presentation last year [2002] at a Foresight Institute conference, a former national security advisor for Vice President Al Gore predicted increased control. "These guys talking here act as though the government is not part of their lives," said Leon Fuerth, now a professor of international affairs at George Washington University. "They may wish it weren't, but it is. As we approach the issues they debated here today, they had better believe that those issues will be debated by the whole country."

Special Interest Groups Get Favors at Society's Expense

Among groups that benefit from nanotech spending, we're starting to see a lot of unhealthy jockeying for position and rent-seeking going on. Rent seeking is obtaining wealth or power through government action. In general, it grants special interests short-term gains at the expense of the long-term economic health of a society.

To bolster its rent-seeking abilities, the Nanobusiness Alliance trade group signed up former House Speaker Newt Gingrich as its chairman and Rep. Robert Walker, former House Science committee chairman, and former Transportation Secretary Rodney Slater as advisors. Corporations that hand over up to $25,000 a year to the alliance can be part of all "legislative tours at no charge" and receive "free access to legislative" lists of key members of Congress and their aides. Alliance members include both startups and the billion-dollar firms Lockheed Martin, Agfa, Gateway, and GE.

Private Funding *Is* Flourishing

If these CEOs viewed nanotech research as too risky to fund themselves, there might be more justification for government dollars. Instead, private investment is flourishing. According to a statement from the Nanobusiness Alliance: "Some of the world's largest companies, including IBM, Motorola, Hewlett Packard, Lucent, Hitachi, Mitsubishi, NEC, Corning, Dow Chemical and 3M have launched significant nanotech initiatives through their own venture capital funds or as a direct result of their own R&D."

A venture capital company devoted exclusively to nanotech, Lux Capital, already exists. Lux Capital estimates that from 1995 to 2000, the number of news articles referencing nanotechnology jumped sixfold, and a billion dollars of venture capital flowed into the nanotech industry last year [2002]. A recent report from the firm said companies are increasingly conducting pure or basic research to keep competitive. . . . Private spending on pure research is supposed to surpass public spending in the next year. Other firms turn to partnerships with academia, essentially outsourcing R&D initiatives.

Evidently, basic research in the case of nanotechnology *can* be funded privately. While a firm may not be able to capitalize on all the benefits of basic research it pays for itself, CEOs seem to believe that a sufficient understanding of the fundamentals leads to applications that can be profitable. . . .

No Justification for Excess Government Funding

Even government officials who argue for more federal spending recognize that the potential payoff for private investors is tremendous. Phillip J. Bond, technology undersecretary at the Commerce Department, predicted in an April 2003 speech that the global market for nano-products would reach $1 trillion by 2015. Bond added: "I for one would bet this is an underestimation. The accelerating rate of the accumulation of knowledge fueled by IT and the collaborative engine of the Internet lead me to conclude that models of the past cannot predict the rate of future advances."

Bond's argument proves too much. If the potential payoff for private investors—$1 trillion is one-tenth of America's current [gross domestic product] GDP—is so huge, the justification for the government's nanotech research spending should be that much smaller.

| "Government intervention turns potential mishaps into disastrous tragedies."

The U.S. Government Should Stay Out of Nanotechnology Research

Sigrid Fry-Revere

In the following viewpoint, Sigrid Fry-Revere asserts that the U.S. government should stay out of nanotechnology research. Fry-Revere believes that the government's only role in nanotechnology research should be "to protect academic freedom, encourage the sharing of information, and enforce informed consent for research subjects." She believes nanotechnology research should stay in the private sector and the government should not promote or regulate any particular type of nanotechnology research for fear of unintended consequences. Fry-Revere uses an example from the past and a depiction of the future to help make her case. Fry-Revere is the former director of bioethics studies at the Cato Institute.

Sigrid Fry-Revere, "Emerging Technologies: A New Era of Regulation," Cato Institute, January 30, 2008. Republished with permission of CATO Institute, conveyed through Copyright Clearance Center, Inc. The CATO Institute is a non-partisan public party research institute and does not endorse any political candidate or political party. www.cato.org.

As you read, consider the following questions:

1. According to Fry-Revere, the movie *Serenity* almost has a cult following among American students interested in what?

2. Why doesn't Fry-Revere think that teenagers' love of the movie *Serenity* reflects a new mistrust of government?

3. According to Fry-Revere, at the beginning of the 20th century, both individuals and governments had their own ideas about how to improve the human gene pool. What did the government do to "improve the gene pool?"

Nigel [Cameron] asked me to give you a sense of the American/libertarian approach to emerging technologies. Let me [begin] by sharing with you some dialogue from a movie that I first learned about from students at a U.S. high school for children gifted in science and technology. The movie is called *Serenity* and it (as well as the T.V. show *Firefly* on which it was based) has almost a cult following among American students interested in science and technology.

A Movie Called *Serenity*

Background: The Earth becomes too crowded and dozens of other planets are terraformed to support human life. The central planets form an Alliance ruled by an interplanetary parliament. The narrator tells us at the beginning of the film that "the Alliance was a beacon of civilization. The savage outer planets were not so enlightened and refused Alliance control." In a war to "ensure a safer universe" the Alliance defeated the Independents. "And, now everyone," the narrator continues, "can enjoy the comfort and enlightenment of true civilization."

First scene: A school classroom: a student asks "Why were the Independents even fighting us? Why wouldn't they want

Thought Control

Serenity shows the propensity for big, intrusive govern-ment to suppress individuality by demanding uniformity of thought. The film opens with a deft satirical jab at progressive education, in which Alliance schoolchildren are being taught how brutish and ugly the outer worlds and their inhabitants are. The teacher, with her soothing voice and appropriately mixed ethnicity, calmly tells chil-dren that The Alliance just wants to provide the frontier with "social and medical advancements." When one stu-dent protests that Alliance control amounts to telling people how to think, the teacher replies, without irony, "We're not telling people what to think—we're just try-ing to show them how."

Peter Suderman, "Spaceships and Small Governments,"
American Spectator, October 11, 2005. http://spectator.org.

to be more civilized?" The heroine answers out of turn, "We meddle. People don't like to be meddled with. We tell them what to do, what to think. Don't run, don't walk. We're in their homes and in their heads and we haven't the right. We're meddlesome." The teacher responds, "We're not telling people what to think . . . we're just trying to show them how."

Scene near the middle of the movie: The heroine and her friends find an outer-planet where everyone is dead. A beacon leads them to a laboratory where they find a recording left be-hind by an Alliance scientist.

Dialogue:

These are just a few of the images we've recorded. And you can see . . . it isn't what we thought. There's been no war here . . . and no terraforming event. The environment is stable. It's the Pax. The G-[exclamation] Paxilon Hydroclorate that we added to the air processors. It was supposed to calm the population, weed out aggression. Well, it works. The people here stopped fighting. And then they stopped everything else. They stopped going to work . . . they stopped breeding, talking, eating. There's a million people here, and they all just let themselves die.

[Crashing] [Gasps] I have to be quick. About a tenth of a percent of . . . the population had the opposite reaction to the Pax. Their aggressor response increased beyond madness. They have become . . . [crashing] Well, they've killed most of us. And not just killed . . . they've done things.

Reavers [monsters that have been attacking settlers] They made them.

I won't live to report this, but people have to know. We meant it for the best . . . to make people safer. [Reavers growling] God! [Woman screaming][Reaver growling]

This movie, so loved by science oriented teenagers all over the U.S., doesn't reflect a new mistrust in government. One of America's founding principles is a mistrust of government. Our constitution contains numerous safeguards to protect individuals against tyranny of the majority and the abuse of power by government officials.

Government's Role in Research

For all of us, emerging technologies conjure up images of both a new enlightenment and the possible destruction of what is most valuable in human nature. Of course, there is also a range of possibilities in between. Talking and thinking about the necessary and sufficient conditions for what it means to be human, as we have done here today, is important, and we should share our insights with the public.

The role governments should play in the development of emerging technology is to protect academic freedom, encourage the sharing of information, and enforce informed consent for research subjects. Governments should not try to assess what types of research are most beneficial to society. There is no shared conception of humanity and not even the wisest men and women could possibly judge for anyone other than themselves whether the use of a particular technology would constitute an affront to their humanity.

The Nobel economist F. A. Hayek in his last book *The Fatal Conceit* argued that human beings are daunted by unintended consequences and that governments that try to regulate human interaction based on broad-scale economic and social predictions are destined to make large mistakes. Applying Hayek's reasoning to emerging technologies means that the best way to ensure caution is to keep government out of the pursuit of scientific knowledge. When governments, which are run by individuals no less fallible than the rest of humanity, make mistakes, those mistakes loom larger than life, affecting not only the lives of the individuals who willingly participated in private experiments, but the lives of whole populations.

A Sad Example

I have time for only one example, but it is a poignant one. At the beginning of the 20th century, eugenics [improving the human race through selective breeding] was touted as the answer to all of humanity's problems. Great scientists such as Alexander Graham Bell and Carl Campbell Brigham (inventor of the SAT test used to test American students for university admissions) at first supported eugenics, as did numerous Nobel Laureates, most European governments, and every U.S. president between 1901 and 1933. Many people all over the world worked hard both in their private lives and through government policy to implement the principles of eugenics.

Both individuals and governments had their own ideas about how to improve the human gene pool. Individuals tried marrying only people they considered superior specimens of humanity. Governments, on the other hand, imposed laws against interracial marriage, sterilized those they believed to be of low intelligence or mentally ill, and even exterminated whole groups of people who because of their race, sexual orientation or religion were thought inferior specimens of humanity. If the eugenics movement had remained in the private sphere, resulting in nothing more than discriminatory marriage practices by some private individuals, the word "eugenics" would be remembered as little more than a silly fad. Instead, governments got involved and now the word "eugenics" is almost synonymous with mass sterilizations and genocide.

Government Should Stay Out of Science

Emerging technologies such as genetic engineering, nanotechnology, mechanical implants, artificial intelligence, and all the others we've discussed today may be the answer to many of humanity's problems. Or, they may be the next eugenics. Government intervention turns potential mishaps into disastrous tragedies. Let's keep government out of science and let the advances and mistakes take place in the private sector where humanity can learn from scientific successes and failures on a manageable scale.

> "Not only can too many regulations strangle innovation in the cradle, but over-regulation can ironically cause under-regulation, leading to safety hazards."

New Nanotechnology Regulations Are Not Urgently Needed

Sonia Arrison

In the following viewpoint, Sonia Arrison argues that nanotechnology does not need new and stronger government oversight. She maintains that over-regulation can stifle new businesses and emerging technologies. Additionally, if regulations are too strong, regulators will be reluctant to enforce them, creating a worse situation. Arrison maintains that safety concerns about nanotechnology are being addressed by scientists and she doesn't think any new regulations are needed to oversee the industry. Arrison, is an author, a TechNewsWorld *columnist, and director of technology studies at the California-based Pacific Research Institute.*

As you read, consider the following questions:

1. What is the name of the director of the National Nano-technology Coordination Office, who Arrison says has taken a "reasonable stand" on nanotechnology regulation?

2. According to Arrison, the state of California released a report brainstorming on how to create what?

3. According to Arrison, the Foresight Institute released guidelines for self-regulation modeled after experience in what field?

Anyone who purchased clear sunscreen or wore stain-resistant pants during the holidays [Christmas] was probably enjoying the benefits of commercialized nanotechnology. While nanotech advances are exciting, some observers dangerously press for greater government oversight in the sector.

Nanotechnology, the manipulation of matter at the molecular level, can create better materials, such as stronger metals and better paints. It also opens the door for self-replicating devices and particles so small that they may enter the bloodstream to help cure disease. This revolution, like any new technology, can be deployed for beneficial or nefarious [evil] purposes.

Greater Regulation of Nanotech Not Reasonable

In a report released this week [January 11, 2006] environmental policy analyst J. Clarence Davies argued for greater regulation of nanotechnology. America's current laws, he says, "either suffer from major shortcomings of legal authority, or from a gross lack of resources, or both." The problem, according to Davies, is that current laws "provide a very weak basis for identifying and protecting the public from potential risk,

Don't Throw a Blanket Over Nanotech

If you would like an example of how business can flourish in a largely unregulated environment, look at the changes to our lives that have occurred thanks to growth of the Internet. E-mail, VoIP, eBay and Google have greatly enhanced lives around the globe. What happens when there is too much regulation? Too often you wind up with tragic corporate sagas and employee fallout. Just look at what is happening to the airline business or to AT&T. Let's not throw a blanket over nanotech before it begins to blossom.

Jose Wolfe, "Nanotech vs. the Green Gang,"
Forbes, April 6, 2005.

especially as nanotechnologies become more complex in structure and function and the applications become more diverse."

Of course, Davies also admits that "we know little about possible adverse effects of nanotechnology." That's partly because of the nascent [emerging] status of the technology and perhaps also because the risks aren't that high. Even government officials seemed surprised at the suggestion of new regulations.

Clayton Teague, director of the National Nanotechnology Coordination Office, told the Associated Press that "Until we have information that there are truly inadequacies in existing regulations, any additional regulations beyond what we already would have would be burdensome to industry and the advancement of the field."

It's encouraging to see national policy makers taking such a reasonable stand. Perhaps that's because they know that advances in nanotechnology will bring greater economic opportunities and tax dollars.

Indeed, it has been estimated that by 2015, the global marketplace for products that use the technology will reach US$1 trillion and employ two million workers. The technology is so promising that the state of California recently released a report brainstorming on how to create a successful Nano-Valley, similar to Silicon Valley, which didn't face regulatory threats in its infancy.

Over-Regulation Is Dangerous

For his part, Davies argues that current levels of government oversight could create distrust and lead to a "public rejection of the technology." While government rules sometimes have a legitimizing effect, that's a poor reason to support them. Over-regulation comes with serious dangers too.

Not only can too many regulations strangle innovation in the cradle, but over-regulation can ironically cause under-regulation, leading to safety hazards. In "Forward to the Future," a Pacific Research Institute report, law professor and celebrity blogger Glenn Reynolds discusses this problem.

"When statutes require especially stringent regulations, administrators will tend not to issue regulations at all. Extraordinarily strict rules on workplace toxins, for example, have led to a failure by the Occupational Safety and Health Administration (OSHA) to address all but a tiny minority of chemicals believed to be toxic." And of course, government rules tend to discourage the creation of private-sector solutions.

Light Regulation Is Best

The scientific community is well aware of the potential dangers with nano-scale particles. The public will be glad to know that the discussion over proper methods is thriving and developing in tandem with the technology. In addition, concerned groups such as the Foresight Institute in California have released guidelines for self-regulation modeled on the extensive experience in biotechnology where there has been great technical progress and little danger to public safety.

Nanotechnology holds much promise for advances in a number of areas such as material science and medicine, but the nascent industry faces threats from those who believe government should solve problems before they occur. Nanotech scientists must be free to develop their products, as well as the rules that govern their development, in order to reap the rewards and protect society from potential pitfalls. The best approach is the light regulation that already exists, combined with a strong scientific culture of self-regulation.

"Industry should not overlook the important powers that the CPSC (Consumer Product Safety Commission) has at its disposal, should nanotechnology employed in consumer products create intolerable risks to human health or safety."

The Government Can Protect the Public from Hazardous Nanotech Products

Jeff Bromme

In the following viewpoint, Jeff Bromme asserts that the U.S. Consumer Product Safety Commission (CPSC) is ready to protect the public from hazardous nanoproducts. The CPSC is a federal agency created in 1972 to protect the American public from unreasonable risks associated with consumer products. According to Bromme, although there is not a lot of activity at the agency in regard to nanotechnology, the agency has the tools and the authority to protect the public from potentially hazardous nanotech products. Bromme describes how the agency can regu-

Jeff Bromme, "Nanotech and the CPSC," *Product Safety & Liability Reporter*, vol. 33, March 14, 2005, pp. 269–294. Copyright © 2005 by The Bureau of National Affairs, Inc., (800-372-1033). All rights reserved. Adapted with permission from Product Safety & Liability Reporter, 33 PSLR 291. www.bna.com.

late nanotechnology using existing U.S. statutes, such as the Federal Hazardous Substances Act and the Poison Prevention Packaging Act. Bromme is an attorney and former general counsel of the Consumer Product Safety Commission.

As you read, consider the following questions:

1. According to Bromme, who coined the term "nanotechnology" and in what year?

2. According to Bromme, how many statutes does the CPSC administer?

3. According to Bromme, which U.S. statute would be useful for regulating nanotechnology that alters the characteristics of fabric?

The Fiscal Year 2006 budget proposal that the Consumer Product Safety Commission [CPSC] submitted to Congress in February [2005] suggests that the agency may be about to launch research in the developing field of nanotechnology. . . .

This is the first budget proposal in which the agency acknowledges that it may begin flexing its regulatory muscles in this emerging field.

What Is Nanotechnology?

Nanotechnology is the "science and technology of building electronic circuits and devices from single atoms and molecules." The federal Office of Management and Budget [OBM] defines nanotechnology as "Research and development at the atomic, molecular, or macromolecular levels, in the length of approximately 1–100 nm [nanometer] range, to provide a fundamental understanding of phenomena and materials at the nanoscale, and to create and use structures, devices, and systems that have novel properties and functions because of their small size." The National Nanotechnology Initiative

("NNI") states a definition that involves each of the following three elements: "1. Research and technology development at the atomic, molecular or macromolecular levels, in the length scale of approximately 1–100 nanometer range. 2. Creating and using structures, devices and systems that have novel properties and functions because of their small and/or intermediate size. 3. Ability to control or manipulate on the atomic scale."

Engineered nanoparticles 1/100,000 the width of a human hair [according to C. Long and B. Beck] "already have a number of significant commercial uses in high-capacity computer drives, automobile catalytic converters, inks, sunscreens, stain-free clothing, and longer-lasting tennis balls." Other products that use nanotechnology include certain paints and coatings, metal-cutting tools, lightweight, stronger tennis rackets, glare-reducing coatings for eyeglasses, dental-bonding agents, and many others. A number of these products fall squarely within the jurisdiction of the CPSC.

In the future, nanoparticles will find expanded uses (i) in making plastics stronger; (ii) enhancing biological imaging for medical diagnostics and drug discovery; (iii) in polymer films in display technology for laptops, cell phones and other uses; (iv) in catalysts, where they can enhance reactions; and (v) in a wide array of pharmaceutical and chemical applications.

The increasing frequency with which nanotechnology is employed commercially comes after at least two decades of basic research. Indeed, the term "Nano-Technology" apparently was created by a professor at Tokyo Science University in 1974, not long after CPSC was created.

Many Examining Risks and Benefits of Nanotechnology

The federal government's role in the field of nanotechnology has become more prominent in recent years. In late 1996, a cross-agency group of federal staffers began to meet informally to discuss plans and programs in the field of nanotechnology. These informal meetings eventually evolved into the Interagency Working Group on Nanotechnology under the National Science and Technology Council. Then, President [Bill] Clinton's 2001 budget submission to Congress "raised nanoscale science and technology to the level of a federal initiative, referring to it as the National Nanotechnology Initiative." The 2004 federal budget included nearly $1 billion for the National Nanotechnology Initiative, with a similar amount budgeted for this fiscal year [2005]. Reflecting greater congressional awareness of and interest in this area, last spring [2004], Senator George Allen (R-Va.) announced the establishment of the Congressional Nanotechnology Caucus.

A survey last year concluded that nearly 800 companies were involved with nanotechnology as of March 2004. Doubtless the figure has grown since then, and various efforts are underway to coordinate industry approaches on nanotechnology. For example, the International Council on Nanotechnology ("ICON") was formed last year [2004]. . . . The group, funded largely by industry and aimed at increasing public trust in nanotechnology, failed in its initial efforts to persuade public interest groups to join, because of their fears that the group would focus more on public relations than in addressing the potential risks of nanotechnology. Nevertheless, ICON claims broad support by industry, nonprofit foundations and governments as it attempts to facilitate a sustainable nanotechnology industry.

In another recent development, the American National Standards Institute ("ANSI"), an organization whose activities often intersect CPSC's, has established the ANSI-Nanotechnology Standards Panel. Formed in August 2004, that panel "will provide the framework within which stakeholders can work cooperatively to promote, accelerate and co-ordinate the timely development of voluntary consensus standards that are intended to meet identified needs related to nanotechnology research, development, and commercialization."

Assessing the potential human health and safety risks that nanotechnology may pose apparently has not kept pace with its commercial development. As recently as last year, the director of the Center for Biological and Environmental Nanotechnology at Rice University observed, "Right now, the toxicological studies of engineered nanomaterials can be counted on one hand, and more ambitious risk assessments are years away." Another commentator [M. Seeley] recently has reported that "[c]urrently there are limited data available for evaluating potential health hazards associated with exposure to nanoparticles." Still a third observer [C. Long] notes, "For nanoparticles, early toxicological studies suggest some indications of potential toxicity, but little is currently known about the relative importance of different exposure pathways and routes and their environmental fate."

Given the complexity of the science surrounding the benefits and risks of nanoparticles and the number of other federal agencies and private sector organizations now examining these issues, it perhaps is not surprising that the CPSC has been relatively quiescent. It is a small agency, and launching a significant nanotechnology risk assessment would stretch its capabilities and resources. However, industry should not overlook the important powers that CPSC has at its disposal, should nanotechnology employed in consumer products create intolerable risks to human health or safety.

How Would CPSC Regulate or Control Nanotechnology in Consumer Products?

The CPSC administers five statutes. Of these, the Federal Hazardous Substances Act ("FHSA") would appear to be the most likely tool for asserting the agency's influence over nanotechnology uses. Pursuant to the FHSA, the CPSC regulates "haz-

CPSC Nanomaterial Statement

The potential safety and health risks of nanomaterials, as with other compounds that are incorporated into consumer products, can be assessed under existing CPSC statutes, regulations and guidelines. Neither the Consumer Product Safety Act (CPSA) nor the Federal Hazardous Substances Act (FHSA) requires the pre-market registration or approval of products. Thus, it is usually not until a product has been distributed in commerce that the CPSC would evaluate a product's potential risk to the public.

Consumer Product Safety Commission,
"CPSC Nanomaterial Statement," CPSC, August 2005.

ardous substances," generally as defined in a two-prong test. Under the first prong, a substance must be toxic, corrosive, an irritant, a strong sensitizer, flammable or combustible, or generate pressure through decomposition, heat, or other means. Under the second prong, such a substance is a "hazardous substance" under the FHSA if it "may cause substantial personal injury or substantial illness during or as a proximate result of any customary or reasonably foreseeable handling or use, including reasonably foreseeable ingestion by children."

Several consequences flow from the characterization of a substance as a "hazardous substance." First, products constituting the "substance" or made using it may require labeling with words such as "WARNING" or "CAUTION," along with an "affirmative statement of the principal hazard or hazards." The FHSA goes on to spell out additional features of the required label. Although the statute provides for exceptions and a variance procedure, the general rule is that hazardous substances must be labeled properly, and no further regulation is required to affect this. Alternatively, if the label set forth in the statute is inadequate in the circumstances, the agency can promulgate a regulation that would vary or alter the statutory label.

If the hazardous substance is not labeled properly, it is considered "misbranded," and those responsible for introducing the "misbranded hazardous substance" into interstate commerce are subject to various penalties, including criminal penalties.

If the hazardous substance is in a toy or other article "intended for use by children," and is "susceptible of access by a child to whom such toy or other article is entrusted," it is deemed to be a banned hazardous substance, and its distribution can likewise give rise to criminal penalties. As with the labeling requirement, this designation is self-executing.

In addition, the FHSA empowers the CPSC to ban a hazardous substance through regulation if it determines that, notwithstanding the required label, the remaining hazard "is such that the objective of the protection of the public health and safety can be adequately served only by keeping such substance, when so intended or packaged [for use in a household], out of the channels of interstate commerce."

CPSC has a variety of remedies at its disposal in the case of a misbranded or banned hazardous substance. It can seek to require the recall of the offending product. It can seize the product in certain circumstances. As noted, the agency also can enforce the FHSA with criminal penalties, including imprisonment. And it may impose civil penalties, which can be substantial. Each product unit (as distinguished from product line) may be deemed subject to a separate penalty, subject to a maximum for "any related series of violations."

Other statutes that CPSC administers may also prove relevant in some circumstances. It is conceivable that the Flammable Fabrics Act ("FFA") may become implicated as nanotechnology is used to alter the characteristics of fabric. The Poison Prevention Packaging Act ("PPPA") could bear upon issues relating to the characteristics of plastic or other materials used for the safe packaging of drugs and other household substances that should be kept away from children. Similarly, the Consumer Product Safety Act ("CPSA"), with its broad reporting and recall provisions, may be implicated in a particular case.

CPSC Ready to Ensure Nanoproduct's Safety

The FHSA and other statutes that CPSC administers are complex. In the space here, it is not possible to discuss all of the potentially relevant features in this legal architecture, particularly when the risks, if any, of nanotechnology do not appear to be well-characterized. However, this brief overview is sufficient to remind industry and CPSC practitioners that although the agency has had a low profile on nanotechnology issues, it could become a potent player should hazards emerge, particularly in consumer products. The agency's recent budget proposal to Congress should be seen as a shot across the bow and provide industry with added reason to ensure that products in which nanotechnology is used do not pose unacceptable risks to consumers.

Periodical Bibliography

The following articles have been selected to supplement the diverse views presented in this chapter.

David Biello
"Government Fails to Assess Potential Dangers of Nanotechnology," *Scientific American*, December 18, 2008. www.sciam.com.

Diana M. Bowman and Graeme A. Hodge
"A Small Matter of Regulation: An International Review of Nanotechnology Regulation," *Columbia Science & Technology Law Review*, January 29, 2007.

Hiawatha Bray
"Cambridge Considers Nanotech Curbs," *Boston Globe*, January 26, 2007. www.boston.com.

Jill M. Buriak
"Nano Facts vs. Nano Fiction," *Canadian Chemical News*, November–December 2004.

Alexander Goho
"Diatom Menagerie," *Science News*, July 17, 2004.

Joy LePree
"Nanotechnology's Got Game," *Product Design & Development*, June 2006.

Alexis Madrigal
"The Chinese Government's Plans for Nanotechnology," *Wired*, February 17, 2008. http://blog.wired.com.

Gary Marchant and Douglas Sylvester
"Transnational Models for Regulation of Nanotechnology," *Journal of Law, Medicine and Ethics*. Winter 2006. http://papers.ssrn.com.

Bart Mongoven
"Nanotechnology and the Regulation of New Technologies," Stratfor.com, August 23, 2007. www.stratfor.com.

Judith Newman and Michael Thompson
"Best Face Forward," *Allure*, December 2008.

Mike Pitkethly
"Nanotechnology, Regulation and the Environment," *Materials Today*, January–February 2009.

For Further Discussion

Chapter 1

1. Roger Whatmore traces the beginnings of nanotechnology to a 1959 lecture given by Richard Feynman, while Adolfo Gutierrez says nanotechnology isn't "new" at all. How does each author support his contention of whether or not nanotechnology is new? Which author do you think provides the best argument?

2. Both Roger Whatmore and Michael Buerger discuss molecular assemblers, or personal nanofactories. Compare and contrast their differing views on the feasibility of this technology, and also the benefits and concerns.

3. Barnaby J. Feder points out the ways that nanotechnology can help the environment, while the Royal Commission says that nanoparticles could pose risks to the environment. Does either author mention the opposing viewpoint, i.e. does Feder refer to the risks of nanotechnology or does the Royal Commission refer to the benefits of nanotechnology?

4. Peter Singer, Fabio Salamanca-Buentello, and Abdallah S. Daar contend that nanotechnology can help people in developing countries, but Georgia Miller and Rye Senjen from the Friends of the Earth argue that nanotechnology will be used for the rich at the expense of the poor. Which viewpoint do you agree with and why?

Chapter 2

1. In his viewpoint, Eric Drexler maintains that molecular manufacturing nanorobots are feasible, practical, and will be part of our future. William Illsey Atkinson, however, thinks Drexler is more of a fraud than a scientific vision-

ary. How would you describe the "tone" of Atkinson's viewpoint and do you think it helped, hurt, or had no impact on the strength of Atkinson's argument? Whose argument do you think was stronger? Support your answer.

2. Steven G. Burgess looks at molecular manufacturing and sees abundance for all of mankind, while Britt Gillette looks at molecular nanotechnology and sees the end of the world. Whose viewpoint do you agree with and why? Use text from the viewpoint to support your answer.

3. James John Bell asserts that there is a real concern that nanotechnology will lead to an event called a singularity. Richard Jones, however, doubts that a singularity will ever occur. What evidence does each author use to support his viewpoint and which set of evidence do you believe is more persuasive and why?

Chapter 3

1. Alan H. Goldstein writes about the ways that nanotechnology will revolutionize medicine, while Kostas Kostarelos says overhyping nanomedicine can do more harm than good. Do you think Kostarelos would characterize Goldstein's viewpoint as more reality or more hype? Support your answer with examples from the text.

2. After reading the viewpoints of Goldstein, Kostarelos, and Raj Bawa and Summer Johnson, what points of agreement can you find among them? Are there common concerns that are found in two, or all three viewpoints, and if so what are they? Do you think Kostarelos would agree with the definition of nanomedicine offered by Bawa and Johnson? Why or why not?

3. George Dvorsky and Nigel Cameron debate the morality of altering human nature with nanomedicine and other nanotechnological devices. What kind(s) of limit(s) do you think Dvorsky and Cameron would propose? For in-

stance, do you think Cameron would want to abolish all use of nanomedicine or just some? Do you think Dvorsky would accept any limits and if so, what kinds? Based on their viewpoints, do you think there is any common ground that will allow Dvorsky and Cameron to work together to set limits on nanotechnology-enabled alteration of human nature?

Chapter 4

1. Jacob Heller and Christine Peterson contend that the government should fund nanotechnology research. Declan McCullagh disagrees. In what ways do you think the government can become involved in and influence nanotechnology research? Use examples from the other viewpoints in the chapter. Do you think the government should stay out of nanotechnology research? Support your answer.

2. Sonia Arrison asserts that new nanotechnology regulations are not necessary. Debates about the appropriate level of regulation of new technologies are common. Provide an example of another "technology," which garnered a great deal of discussion about the need for regulations. What do you think about the need for new nanotechnology regulations?

3. Jeff Bromme says that the Consumer Products Safety Commission (CPSC) can protect the public from nanohazards contained in consumer products. What is his primary basis for his position? Do you agree with his argument?

Organizations to Contact

The editors have compiled the following list of organizations concerned with the issues debated in this book. The descriptions are derived from materials provided by the organizations. All have publications or information available for interested readers. The list was compiled on the date of publication of the present volume; the information provided here may change. Be aware that many organizations take several weeks or longer to respond to inquiries, so allow as much time as possible.

ASME Nanotechnology Institute
Three Park Avenue, New York, NY   10016
(212) 591-7789
e-mail: nano@asme.org
Web site: http://nano.asme.org

The ASME Nanotechnology Institute is a professional society composed of engineers, scientists, finance and business professionals, government leaders, and students dedicated to furthering the art, science, and practice of nanotechnology. The institute is a clearinghouse for ASME activities in nanotechnology and provides interdisciplinary programs and activities to bridge science, engineering, and applications.

Center for Policy on Emerging Technologies (C-PET)
10 G Street NE, Washington, DC   20002
(202) 248-5027
e-mail: info@c-pet.org
Web site: www.c-pet.org

The Center for Policy on Emerging Technologies (C-PET) is a Washington, D.C.-based science and technology think tank. C-PET studies nanotechnologies, biotechnologies, information technologies, and other emerging technologies that have the potential to profoundly affect society. The C-PET Emerging Technologies group is a public listserv that delivers daily news and comments on the latest technological developments.

Center For Responsible Nanotechnology (CRN)
213 Eastern Parkway, Suite 11, Brooklyn, NY 11238
(718) 398-7272
e-mail: info@CRNano.org
Web site: www.crnano.org

The Center for Responsible Nanotechnology (CRN) is a nonprofit organization whose mission is to raise awareness of the benefits, dangers, and possibilities for responsible use of advanced nanotechnology; to expedite a thorough examination of the environmental, humanitarian, economic, military, political, social, medical, and ethical implications of molecular manufacturing; and to assist in the creation and implementation of wise, comprehensive, and balanced plans for responsible worldwide use of this transformative technology. The CRN Web site provides background and educational information about nanotechnology, a blog, and the *C-R-Newsletter*.

Foresight Institute
1455 Adams Drive, Suite 2160, Menlo Park, CA 94025
(650) 289-0860 • fax: (650) 289-0863
e-mail: foresight@foresight.org
Web site: www.foresight.org

The Foresight Institute is a nonprofit public foundation with the goal of promoting beneficial nanotechnology. The institute seeks to promote the beneficial use of nanotechnology to address global challenges, such as providing clean water, preserving the environment, and enabling space development. The institute provides information to help society understand and prepare for nanotechnology through public policy activities, publications, guidelines, networking events, tutorials, conferences, roadmaps, and prizes. The organization publishes various white papers, other publications, and the *Foresight Institute Weekly News Digest*, which features news, lectures, and other information on nanotechnology.

Humanity+: World Transhumanist Association (WTA)
PO Box 128, Willington, CT   06279
(800) 297-2376
e-mail: secretary/at/transhumanism.org
Web site: www.wta.org

Humanity+: World Transhumanist Association (WTA) is an international nonprofit membership organization that advocates the ethical use of technology to expand human capacities. The organization supports the development of and access to new technologies that enable everyone to enjoy better minds, better bodies, and better lives. Humanity+: WTA focuses its activities on how emerging technologies, such as nanotechnology, impact the rights of person, enable people to live longer and better lives, and provide a future-friendly culture. The organization publishes a periodical magazine called *H+*, which covers technological, scientific, and cultural trends that have the potential to change human beings in fundamental ways.

Institute for Molecular Manufacturing (IMM)
555 Bryant Street, Suite 354, Palo Alto, CA   94301
(650) 917-1120 • fax (650) 917-1120
e-mail: admin@imm.org
Web site: www.imm.org

The Institute for Molecular Manufacturing (IMM) conducts and funds nanotechnology research as a complement to its sister organization, the Foresight Institute, which serves an important educational role for nanotechnology. IMM's mission is to enable and conduct research on molecular systems engineering, perform safeguard design, and promote guidelines for research and development practices that will minimize risk from accidental misuse and intentional abuse. The organization sponsors a number of publications including the textbooks *Nanosystems* and *Nanomedicine*.

International Council on Nanotechnology (ICON
Rice University, Houston, TX   77251-1892

(713) 348-8210 • fax: (713) 348-8218
e-mail: colvin@rice.edu
Web site: www.icon.rice.edu

The International Council on Nanotechnology (ICON) is an international, multi-stakeholder organization whose mission is to develop and communicate information regarding potential environmental and health risks of nanotechnology, thereby fostering risk reduction while maximizing societal benefit. ICON sponsors forums and events to explore health and environmental risk issues in nanotechnology, provides information to decision makers, and provides an electronic knowledge base for accessing peer-reviewed publications in nanotechnology. ICON publishes an electronic journal, the *Virtual Journal of Nantoechnology, Environment, Health and Safety*, available at www.icon.rice.edu/virtualjournal.cfm.

The Lifeboat Foundation
1638 Esmeralda Avenue, Minden, NV   89423
(775) 329-0180 • fax: (775) 329-0190
e-mail: lifeboat@lifeboat.com
Web site: http://lifeboat.com

The Lifeboat Foundation is a nonprofit, nongovernmental organization dedicated to encouraging scientific advancements while helping humanity survive existential risks and possible misuse of increasingly powerful technologies, including genetic engineering, nanotechnology, and robotics/artificial intelligence. The Lifeboat Foundation believes that, in some situations, it might be feasible to relinquish technological capacity in the public interest. The organization pursues a variety of options to help humanity survive an existential risk, including helping to accelerate the development of technologies to protect humanity against existential risk, including effective nanotechnological defensive strategies, and even self-sustaining space colonies in case the other defensive strategies fail. The organization publishes a monthly newsletter, called *Lifeboat News*.

The Nanoethics Group
California Polytechnic State University
San Luis Obispo, CA   93407
(805) 756-1111
e-mail: hello@nanoethics.org
Web site: www.nanoethics.org

The Nanoethics Group is a research and education organization composed of professional ethicists. The organization does not promote, nor oppose nanotechnology, but seeks to objectively evaluate key nanotechnology issues by considering all sides of the debate. The organization also actively seeks to help ordinary people, students, and policy makers to understand the issues arising from nanotechnology. The Nanoethics Group has published two anthologies *Nanoethics: The Ethical And Social Implications of Nanotechnology* and *Nanotechnology & Society: Current and Emerging Ethical Issues*, which are frequently used as college textbooks.

National Nanotechnology Initiative (NNI)
National Nanotechnology Coordination Office
Arlington, VA   22230
(703) 292-8626 • fax: (703) 292-9312
e-mail: info@nnco.nano.gov
Web site: www.nano.gov

The National Nanotechnology Initiative (NNI) is a multi-agency U.S. government research and development program. The mission of the NNI is to advance nanotechnology research, to foster the transfer of new nanotechnologies into products for commercial and public benefit, to develop nanotechnology educational resources and a skilled workforce, and to support the responsible development of nanotechnology. The NNI offers several publications, presentations, brochures, a newsletter, and weekly listings of nanotechnology stories and links.

Project on Emerging Nanotechnologies (PEN)
Woodrow Wilson International Center for Scholars
Washington, DC   20004-3027
(202) 691-4282 • fax: (202) 691-4001
e-mail: nano@wilsoncenter.org
Web site: www.nanotechproject.org

The Project on Emerging Nanotechnologies (PEN), a partnership between the Woodrow Wilson International Center for Scholars and the Pew Charitable Trusts, is a nonprofit organization dedicated to helping ensure that as nanotechnologies advance, possible risks are minimized, public and consumer engagement remains strong, and the potential benefits of new nanotechnologies are realized. The PEN collaborates with researchers, government, industry, nongovernmental organizations (NGOs), policy makers, and others to look long term, to identify gaps in knowledge and regulatory processes, and to develop strategies for closing them. The PEN publishes its research results, reports, and the outcomes of meetings. Recent publications include *Nanotechnology: The Social and Ethical Issues* and *A Hard Pill to Swallow: Barriers to Effective FDA Regulation of Nanotechnology-Based Dietary Supplements*.

Richard E. Smalley Institute for Nanoscale Science and Technology
PO Box 1892, MS-100, Houston, TX   77251-1892
(713) 348-2980 • fax: (713) 348-5320
e-mail: nano@rice.edu
Web site: http://smalley.rice.edu

The Richard E. Smalley Institute for Nanoscale Science and Technology is named after and was founded by the Nobel prize winning Smalley, who lost his life to cancer on October 28, 2005. The mission of the Smalley Institute is to support and promote researchers using nanotechnology to tackle civilization's grand challenges, such as energy, water, environment, disease, and education. The Institute focuses on education, research, community programs, corporate partnerships, and government relations. FAQs and educational publications are available on Institute's Web site.

U.S. Consumer Product Safety Commission(CPSC)
4330 East West Highway, Bethesda, MD   20814
(301) 504-7923 • fax: (301) 504-0124
e-mail: http://www.cpsc.gov/cgibin/info.aspx
Web site: www.cpsc.gov

The U.S. Consumer Product Safety Commission (CPSC) is the federal agency charged with ensuring that consumer products are safe. The CPSC works to protect consumers and families from products that pose a fire, electrical, chemical, or mechanical hazard or can injure children. The CPSC also works to ensure the safety of consumer products such as toys, cribs, power tools, cigarette lighters, and household chemicals. CPSC reports on the safety of consumer products such as toys, pools, all-terrain vehicles, and many others are available on its Web site.

Bibliography

Books

Fritz Allhoff and Patrick Lin, eds.	*Nanotechnology and Society: Current and Emerging Ethical Issues.* New York: Springer, 2008.
Fritz Allhoff, Patrick Lin, James Moor, and John Weckert, eds.	*Nanoethics: The Ethical and Societal Implications of Nanotechnology.* Hoboken, NJ: John Wiley & Sons, 2007.
William Illsey Atkinson	*Nanocosm: Nanotechnology and the Big Changes Coming from the Inconceivably Small.* New York: AMACOM, 2005.
David H. Berube	*Nano-Hype: The Truth Behind the Nanotechnology Buzz.* New York: Prometheus Books, 2005.
Damien Broderick	*Year Million: Science at the Far Edge of Knowledge.* New York: Atlas & Co., 2008.
Eric Drexler	*Engines of Creation.* New York: Fourth Estate, 1996.
Steven A. Edwards	*The Nanotech Pioneers: Where Are They Taking Us?* Hoboken, NJ: Wiley-VCH, 2006.
Ira Flatow	*Present at the Future: From Evolution to Nanotechnology, Candid and Controversial Conversations on Science and Nature.* New York: Collins, 2007.

Nancy Forbes	*Imitation of Life: How Biology Is Inspiring.* Cambridge, MA: MIT Press, 2004.
Lynn Foster	*Nanotechnology: Science, Innovation and Opportunity.* Upper Saddle River, NJ: Prentice Hall, 2006.
James Gardner	*The Intelligent Universe.* Franklin Lakes, NJ: New Page Books, February 2007.
David Goodsell	*Bionanotechnology: Lessons from Nature.* Hoboken, NJ: Wiley-Liss, 2004.
J. Storrs Hall	*Nanofuture: What's Next for Nanotechnology.* Amherst, NY: Prometheus Books, 2005.
David Hambling	*Weapons Grade: Holy Modern Warfare Gave Birth to Our High-Tech World.* New York: Carroll & Graf, 2005.
Geoffrey Hunt and Michael D. Mehta	*Nanotechnology Risk, Ethics and Law.* London: Earthscan, 2006.
Richard A.L. Jones	*Soft Machines: Nanotechnology and Life.* Oxford: Oxford University Press, 2004.
Barbara Karn, Tina Masciangioli, Wei-xian Zhang, Vicki Colvin, and Paul Alivisatos, eds.	*Nanotechnology and the Environment.* Washington, DC: American Chemical Society, 2004.

Ray Kurzweil   *The Singularity Is Near: When Humans Transcend Biology.* New York: Viking, 2005.

Michael Mandel   *Rational Exuberance: Silencing the Enemies of Growth and Why the Future Is Better than You Think.* New York: HarperBusiness, 2004.

Andrew Maynard   *Nanotechnology: A Research Strategy for Addressing Risk.* Washington, DC: Woodrow Wilson International Center for Scholars, 2006.

Wil McCarthy   *Hacking Matter: Levitating Chairs, Quantum Mirages, and the Infinite Weirdness of Programmable Atoms.* New York: Basic Books, 2003.

Bill McKibben   *Enough: Staying Human in an Engineered Age.* New York: Times Books, 2003.

Douglas Mulhall   *Our Molecular Future: How Nanotechnology, Robotics, Genetics and Artificial Intelligence Will Transform Our World.* Amherst, NY: Prometheus Books, 2002.

Ramez Naam   *More than Human.* New York: Broadway, 2005.

Daniel Ratner and Mark A. Ratner   *Nanotechnology and Homeland Security.* Upper Saddle River, NJ: Prentice Hall Professional Technical Reference, 2004.

Mihail C. Roco and William Sims Bainbridge
Societal Implications of Nanoscience and Nanotechnology. Boston: Kluwer Academic Publishers, 2001.

Rudy Rucker
Postsingular. New York: Tor, 2007.

Ted Sargent
The Dance of Molecules: How Nanotechnology Is Changing Our Lives. New York: Thunder's Mouth Press, 2006.

Alex Steffen
Worldchanging: A User's Guide for the 21st Century. New York: Abrams, 2006.

Linda Williams and Wade Adams
Nanotechnology Demystified. New York: McGraw-Hill, 2007.

Michael Wilson, Kamali Kannangara, Geoff Smith, and Michelle Simmons
Nanotechnology: Basic Science and Emerging Technologies. Boca Raton, FL: CRC Press, 2002.

Index

A

Abundance potential, 121–126

Abuses of power. *See* Power, abuses

Academic freedom, 231, 234

Access, health care. *See* Health care divide

Action Group on Erosion, Technology and Concentration, 89, 91

Addiction, drugs, 50

Advanced Cell Technology (company), 144–145

Aeronautical engineering, 116

Africa, 78, 79, 83, 90

Agricultural productivity
    enhancement, developing nations, 77–78
    Industrial Revolution, 52–53

Airbots, 174

Aircraft, 146

Allen, George, 245

American National Standards Institute (ANSI), 245–246

American Physical Society, Feynman lecture, 14, 22, 25–26, 27, 102

"The Android and the Human" (speech, Dick), 144

Animal extinction, 149

Antibacterial consumer products, 19, 60

Antichrist, 127–128, 135

Apocalypse, 127–135

Arms races
    biorobotics, 147, 148
    weapons, 127, 129–133

Arrison, Sonia, 237–241

Art and nanomedicine, 203, 205

Artificial intelligence, 124
    defenses, 99
    existential risks, 55, 98, 132
    surveillance, 134
    takeover/"Singularity," 136, 137, 138, 141, 142, 153

Artificial organs, 148, 155

Asbestos, 34

Asia, water, 78

Assemblers
    cause of job losses, 94–95
    challenges in creating, 151–152, 153–154, 155
    descriptions, 28–29, 103–105, 112
    fears, 23, 33–34, 44, 47–53, 106, 129–130
    medical device production, 174
    nanofactory basics, 51, 154–155
    providers of abundance, 121–122, 123–124, 125, 145

Assessment groups, 82

Atkinson, William Illsey, 109–120

Atomic force microscope, 14, 17

Atomic weapons. *See* Nuclear technologies/weapons

Atoms
    manipulation, 27–28
    microscope views, 14

health and environmental impacts, nanoparticles, 21, 35, 64–72, 246

long-term research needs, 67–69, 70, 72, 149, 187, 194–195, 207

research standardization need, 71

Results, lack in nanotechnology, 40, 41–42, 160, 222

Revelation (book, Bible), 127–128, 135

Revolution in everything (RIE). *See* Societal transformation

Revolutionization of medicine, 168–180, 185, 189

Reynolds, Glenn, 240

Ribosomes, 103, 156

Rich-poor divide

health care, 174, 180, 194, 202–203

human enhancement, 202, 209

nanotechnology can improve, 73–83, 121–126, 199

nanotechnology will not improve, 36, 53–54, 84–95, 124, 209

Rigidity requirements, 120, 151–152, 157, 159–160

RipeSense, 20

Robot-human interaction, 92, 93, 144–146

Robots

biorobots, 137, 147, 154

defensive, 99–100, 146–147

humanness, 144, 145–146

medical, cancer treatments, 172–173

medical, cryogenics, 166–167

medical, realism questioned, 160, 181, 182, 186

medical, transhumanist predictions, 112, 120, 145, 174, 175

nano-manufacturing, 26–27, 28, 99–100, 112–115

traditional manufacturing, 104, 114–115

Rohrer, Heinrich, 16

Rostand, Jean, 165

Royal Commission on Environmental Pollution, 64–72

R.U.R. (Capek), 145–146

Ruska, Ernst, 15

Russia, 219

S

Safety concerns. *See* Environmental impacts; Health and safety concerns

Salamanca-Buentello, Fabio, 73–83

Sargent, John F., 219

Scanning probe microscope, 27–28

Scanning tunneling microscope, 14, 16, 107, 153, 155

Scarcity, 121–122, 123, 124, 152

Schermer, Michael, 167

Science fiction

literature examples, 29, 34, 99, 144, 145–146

military technology comparisons, 36, 146–147

nanomedicine overhype comparisons, 181, 184, 186

Scientific research principles, 117–118

Self-programming, 124

Self-protection, 99–100, 132

Self-regulation, 240–241, 245–246

Self-replication, 28–29, 98–100, 112, 129, 143, 155, 199

Sematech, 224–225
Semiconductor industry, 27, 139
Semiconductor properties, 29–30
Senjen, Rye, 84–95
Serenity (film), 232–234
Sheahen, Laura, 198–204, 205–210
Short-term profits, 126
Singer, Peter, 73–83, 192
Single-atom manipulation, 27–28
Singularity
    nanotechnology will contribute, 136–150
    nanotechnology will not contribute, 151–162
Site licenses, 48
6th Framework Programme, 81
Skepticism, 87
    Drexlerian theories, 113, 117–120
    nanocryonics, 167
    nanomedicine, 181, 184, 185–186
    See also Cynicism
Slater, Rodney, 228
Slow-release properties, 77–78
Smalley, Richard, 30, 33, 114
Social marginalization, 53–54
Societal transformation
    developing nations, potential, 75–79, 86
    Industrial Revolution, 45, 52–53, 85, 89
    nanotechnology potential, 46, 85, 86–87, 92–95, 112
    "Singularity," 136–150, 152–153
Soil
    pollution cleanup, 59, 62, 79
    productivity enhancement, 77
Solar energy, 76–77, 106, 161, 218
Soot, 30, 35

South Korea, 218, 219
Special interest groups, 225–226, 227, 228–229
Spending, research and development. *See* Funding
Spin logic, 26
Stain-resistant products, 19, 224
Standardization, research, 71
Stem cell research, 227–228
Sterilization, eugenic, 236
"Sticky fingers" problem, 27, 33
Stiff-arm nanomanipulator, 115–116
Storage
    energy, 76–77
    information, vastness, 33, 141, 196
Suderman, Peter, 233
Suffering and empathy, 203
Sun Microsystems, 139, 142–143
Sunscreens, 30, 35, 207, 224
Supercomputers, 141
Surface properties, nanoparticles, 30, 66, 159
Surveillance
    military, 146
    robotic, 134–135, 148
    societal, 87, 134–135, 200, 207
Suspended animation. *See* Cryogenics
Sustainability, economic, 76, 80

T

Taiwan, 218, 219
Taniguchi, Norio, 26
Targeted drug delivery. *See* Drug delivery technologies
Targeted medicine, 176–180
Teague, Clayton, 239